THE CONGRESS OF VIENNA

In 1814–15, after the French Revolutionary and Napoleonic Wars, the leaders of the most important countries in Europe gathered together to redraw the frontiers of their continent. In *The Congress of Vienna*, Tim Chapman explores the attempt by Britain, Russia, Austria and Prussia to agree Europe's new frontiers after almost twenty years of continuous fighting against France.

The Congress of Vienna offers a readable introduction to this difficult topic, providing

- a background to the negotiations from the time of the French Revolution
- a summary of the agreements reached
- assessment of the longer-term consequences
- analysis of the success of the Congress

The author traces the survival and evolution of the Vienna settlement through many revolutions and explains its eventual demise with the emergence of modern Europe.

Tim Chapman teaches History at Wisbech Grammar School.

D0905791

THE CONGRESS OF VIENNA

Origins, processes and results

Tim Chapman

London and New York

First published 1998
by Routledge
11 New Fetter Lane, London EC4P 4EE

Simultaneously published in the USA and Canada
by Routledge
29 West 35th Street, New York, NY 10001

Typeset in Bembo by
J&L Composition Limited, Filey, North Yorkshire
Printed and bound in Great Britain by Clays Ltd, St Ives PLC

British Library Cataloguing in Publication Data
A catalogue record for this book is available
from the British Library

Library of Congress Cataloguing in Publication Data
Chapman, Tim, 1964–
The Congress of Vienna: origins, processes, and results/
Tim Chapman.
p.   cm
Includes bibliographical references and index.
ISBN 0–415–17993–9 (hbk.).—ISBN 0–415–17994–7 (pbk.)
1. Congress of Vienna (1814–1815) 2. Napoleonic Wars, 1800–1815
—Influence. 3. Napoleonic Wars, 1800–1815—Treaties. I. Title.
DC249.C48   1998
940.2′7—dc21   98–11040
CIP

ISBN 0–415–17993–9 (hbk)
ISBN 0–415–17994–7 (pbk)

TO MY EUROPEAN HISTORY
STUDENTS, 1989–98

CONTENTS

CONTENTS

FIGURES, MAPS
AND TABLES

Figures

Maps

Tables

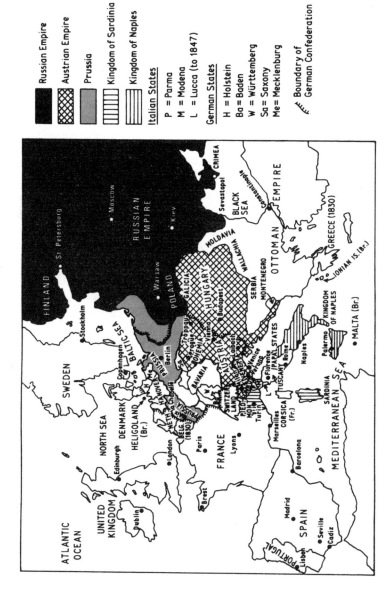

Europe 1815–48.

Legend:

- Russian Empire
- Austrian Empire
- Prussia
- Kingdom of Sardinia
- Kingdom of Naples

Italian States
- P = Parma
- M = Modena
- L = Lucca (to 1847)

German States
- H = Holstein
- Ba = Baden
- W = Württemberg
- Sa = Saxony
- Me = Mecklenburg

- Boundary of German Confederation

Map labels:

ATLANTIC OCEAN
UNITED KINGDOM
Edinburgh
Dublin
London
NORTH SEA
DENMARK
Copenhagen
HELIGOLAND (Br.)
SWEDEN
Stockholm
BALTIC SEA
FINLAND
St Petersburg
RUSSIAN EMPIRE
Moscow
Kiev
Warsaw
POLAND
GALICIA
Berlin
PRUSSIA
HANOVER
NETH.
BELG. (1830)
Brest
Paris
Lyons
FRANCE
SWITZERLAND
Marseilles
CORSICA (Fr.)
SPAIN
Madrid
Seville
Cadiz
Barcelona
PORTUGAL
Lisbon
MEDITERRANEAN SEA
SARDINIA
Turin
PIED.
Florence
TUSCANY
PAPAL STATES
Rome
Venice
Milan
Trieste
Laibach
Vienna
BOHEMIA
Prague
AUSTRIA
HUNGARY
Budapest
MOLDAVIA
WALLACHIA
SERBIA
MONTENEGRO
OTTOMAN EMPIRE
Constantinople
GREECE (1830)
IONIAN IS. (Br.)
KINGDOM OF NAPLES
Naples
Palermo
MALTA (Br.)
BLACK SEA
Sevastopol
CRIMEA
BAVARIA
WISSUA

1

WAR AND REVOLUTION
IN EUROPE 1789–1814

The Congress of Vienna was a gathering of all the major states of
Europe to draw up a peace settlement at the end of the wars
against Napoleon in 1814–15. It was attended by the four main
allies – Britain, Russia, Austria and Prussia – which were the
countries mostly responsible for the defeat of Napoleonic France,
the state that had caused the wars. Several minor states that had
fought with the victorious allies – such as Spain, Portugal and
Sweden – were also present and most of the remaining countries
of Europe sent delegations.

Importance and scope of the Congress of Vienna

It was one of the most important meetings in European history,
comparable to the Versailles peace conferences after the First World
War or, earlier, the Treaty of Utrecht (1714). It not only set out the
way in which France was to be treated after launching twenty years
of war following the 1789 Revolution and the subsequent rise of
Napoleon; it reconstructed the frontiers of states that spread across
the central and eastern areas of the continent and restored many of
the former rulers. It also set out the fate of a great many colonies
around the world. There was a huge amount at stake.

Some countries that had been invaded and abolished by Napoleon
never reappeared; others were recast in larger or smaller forms while
at the same time the largest states looked for bounty and rewards for
having won the war. In the complex discussions that took place at
Vienna there was a battle for the principles upon which the new
Europe was to be based. And, in the midst of this conference of
power-brokers, there was one of the most glittering displays of
Society figures and leading members of the aristocracy ever seen
on the continent.

It was a momentous occasion and one that turned out to be highly successful. It played a major part in making 1815 a turning-point in European history as a long period of war was brought to a close and it was followed by almost a century of peace. The next general war between Europe's leading states was the Great War of 1914–18. Many students of European history in the nineteenth century begin in 1815, in line with much of the historiography of the period; after all, the map of Europe that emerged in 1815 was the starting-point for great changes later in the century that were wrought by the unification of Italy and Germany.

However, setting 1815 as the point to begin a course is in many ways misleading because it marked above all the end of an era, not the start of a new one. The peacemakers of 1815 were men who were backward-looking and conservative, who were concerned to put right the mistakes and misdeeds of the past that they themselves had witnessed and fought against. Their view was coloured by their own bitter experience of war and revolution. They did not see their task as being to reinvent Europe for the future or to pander to the dangerous new ideas that the French Revolution had spread; rather, they wanted to restore Europe to peace by inflicting limits on France and by strengthening their own defences. They did not want a new Europe so much as a better version of the old one.

In order to understand the Congress of Vienna, then, it is essential briefly to retrace the key developments in Europe from 1789 that informed the peace of 1815. As the peacemakers themselves saw the situation, there were two basic problems. First, they had to contend with the ideas of the French Revolution as they had begun to take root in the populations that the French had conquered, and especially within France itself. Second, they had to find ways to restrict the possibility of France (or any other state) mounting another war as devastating as the last. Of the two problems, the second was the one that they took most seriously at Vienna, partly because it was the one that, in practical terms, they could do most to combat. It was to be left to the rulers of individual states to deal with internal problems.

The French Revolution

By tradition, the French Revolution has been portrayed as the storming of the Bastille on 14 July 1789. This is at best a shorthand explanation for the huge changes in France from the 1780s until the execution of King Louis XVI in 1793. Historical research has shown that there was not just one outbreak of revolution but a series of rebellions against the king and the old system of rule (called the *ancien régime*) by different classes of people and for different reasons. The cumulative effect of these protests was for confrontation and then conflict to emerge with the king, and this situation, initially led by the nobility, developed its own momentum and subsequently revolutionised France. This had not been the aim of the nobility's original protests against the king.

The first group of people in France to rebel against the king was the nobility. In the eighteenth century, its members enjoyed privileges that the ordinary people in society did not share. The nobles were spared paying certain taxes, such as the *taille* on land, and they enjoyed legal advantages in law courts. But from 1787 they became increasingly hostile towards the king because Louis XVI wanted to tax them more heavily. He had to do this in order to pay the debts he had accumulated by fighting in such wars as the American War of Independence, when France helped the USA throw off British rule after 1776. By 1786, the monarchy was on the verge of bankruptcy with a deficit between income and expenditure of 112 million livres.

Louis tried to win over the nobles and raise more income by using some of their own representative bodies. He recalled the Assembly of Notables, a dormant assembly of noblemen and clergy that had last met in 1626, and the Paris Parlement which was one of thirteen courts responsible for administering much of France. At different times, they were each asked to support tax rises in return for Louis passing reforms in other areas of French life, such as the legal system, education and the church. However, neither the Assembly nor the Parlement were won over by this royal ploy, and each had the same response; Louis had to allow the Estates-General to meet.

The Estates-General was effectively a parliament that was elected by all members of French society — which meant the peasants and workers as well as the clergy and nobility. The debate between Louis and the nobles was clearly developing beyond the problem of tax to wider issues in society. Louis was therefore reluctant to call the Estates-General and initially reacted by cutting back the powers of the parlements. However, by August 1788 the royal coffers were empty and, desperate to raise more revenue, Louis gave in and called the Estates-General. The revolt of the nobles was by this stage well under way.

The second group of people to rebel against the king was the bougeoisie or middle class which had hitherto supported the opposition of the nobles. It became rebellious when it seemed that the Estates-General would meet on the same basis as in the past (though it had not met since 1614). This meant that its members would mostly be the nobles and clergy who might work only for their own benefit rather than for the good of the French people as a whole. The vast majority of the population was composed of peasants, together with urban workers and the middle class, and by 1789 these groups were seriously underrepresented in the Estates-General. The bourgeoisie led the opposition to the aristocrats and campaigned for better representation. Eventually, they were successful and in the elections that followed there were 610 deputies to represent the ordinary people compared to 303 for the clergy and just 282 for the nobility.

All of this was a circuitous route for the monarchy to take simply to raise more money, but by allowing the Estates-General to meet there was now much more at stake. The debate had extended beyond tax and reform to the political importance of ordinary people as well as to the role of the nobles and the king. The assembly first met on 5 May 1789 and its business was pushed along by the bourgeoisie which, on behalf of all of the ordinary people, insisted on joint meetings with the nobles and clergy. The king opposed this because the Estates-General was beginning to evolve independently and represented a challenge to him. Louis' handling of the situation was poor and, after hurried meetings and the 'Tennis Court Oath', the assembly was provoked into full-blooded support for a constitution which would formally limit royal power.

Observers thought that the way was now clear for the king and the Estates-General to reach some agreement about taxation and reform. This turned out not to be the case. Louis was simply buying time before trying to retake all power for himself. He built up the number of troops in and around Paris from 4,000 to over 30,000 in early July 1789 and on 11 July he dismissed one of the ordinary people's leaders, Necker. This inflamed the temper of the Parisian crowds and set the scene for the infamous storming of the Bastille.

The storming of the Bastille

The storming of the Bastille brought in to the course of the French Revolution the third group in French society to rebel against the king. Already, the nobles and bourgeoisie had acted with contributions at a high governmental level. The ordinary people of Paris, the *sans-culotte(s)* or 'the mob' now played a part by seizing weapons and ammunition from gunsmiths so as to take on the royal troops by brute force if necessary. Their motivation was not just political. France, and Paris in particular, was suffering very high grain prices following a succession of poor harvests from 1778 which intensified in 1786 and 1788. The vast majority of workers' pay was spent on bread, the basic foodstuff, and the number of people who were underemployed or out of work altogether was high. Customs posts on the edge of Paris were attacked by mobs for impounding grain and then on 14 July 1789 the mob looted muskets before marching on the Bastille so as to seize ammunition.

The Bastille was an old and notorious prison that had come to symbolise royal power – and cruelty. It contained just seven inmates but the mob was primarily interested in taking hold of its store of gunpowder rather than freeing those inside. By July 1789, many of the royal troops were becoming unreliable and had been moved to the outskirts of Paris thereby leaving the Bastille defended by just thirty Swiss guards and eighty army pensioners. The governor of the Bastille, the Marquis de Launay, appreciated how weak his forces were and eventually surrendered in the hope of avoiding bloodshed. He misjudged the situation and paid with his life, as he was quickly decapitated and his head paraded through the city streets on a pole. While these events did not necessarily mean the end of the French monarchy, they symbolised the shift in power away from the king and towards the people of Paris. By mid-July, about 250,000 Parisians were armed, while the king's troops remained on the edge of town, not trusted by their officers to be loyal to the crown. The revolt of townspeople spread from Paris to other major cities in France, such as Marseilles, Lille and Lyon. This was known as the 'municipal revolution'.

The fourth group to rebel was amongst the most conservative in French society and consisted of the rural labourers. Across most of France, peasants rose up and seized grain held by their local lords and destroyed records of their feudal dues and tithes. Hundreds of chateaux were attacked during the spring and summer of 1789 and the peasants' anger was exacerbated by rumours that the 1789 harvest was going to be deliberately destroyed by groups of men in the pay of the nobles. Although this reaction, known as the 'Great Fear', was not justified, it led to further attacks on the nobility and its property. Clearly, the four rebel groups were not united, as they began to attack each other, but the movement of reform begun by the nobles was now beyond their control and tending towards revolution.

The fall of the monarchy

Louis XVI was in a weak position and had moved his court away from the centre of Paris. On 17 July 1789 he was humiliated when he was brought back to the capital and forced to wear the revolutionary colours of red, white and blue. Effective power now lay with the ordinary people, whose representative body took the name of National Constituent Assembly, and whose aim was at this time to return the country to some sort of calm. Its first step in this direction was the August Decrees which abolished the feudal system and its heavy toll of taxes, tithes and labour dues that fell on the peasantry. This undermined the position of the landlord class and prompted many to leave the country for fear of peasant violence. But it also won over most of the French people to the new Assembly, and enabled it to pass further reforms. With careers becoming open to talent, the bourgeoisie was also won over and it was this group that benefited most from the restructuring of France's institutions in local government, law, the church and the armed forces.

The Assembly had begun its work of modernisation with the famous Declaration of the Rights of Man and the Citizen in August 1789 which began by asserting that 'Men are born free and equal in their rights'. From this followed civil and religious freedoms and the task of devising a constitution to formally limit the king's power. Initially, the Assembly hoped to work with the king, but continuing violence and food shortages in Paris meant that the mob had the final say in what changes were made. Thus, the king was brought back to Paris for a second time in October by a crowd of angry women, and he was effectively held there as a prisoner. The Assembly, too, needed to be mindful of the views of the mob, lest a crowd stormed into one of its meetings and imposed its will by violence – something that was frequently threatened.

The reforms that were passed included the reorganisation of France into departements, districts and communes so that power was decentralised; from 1791, taxation was based primarily on land, although revenue was also raised by confiscating and then selling church lands; trade was speeded up by the introduction of decimal weights and measures, and internal customs barriers were ended in October 1790. Law courts were restructured and made common to the whole of France, and punishments became more humane with the abolition of torture and fewer capital offences; the church was subjected to the Civil Constitution of the Clergy which cut the Pope's influence and realigned the church districts with those of the state. The Catholic Church rejected the change and gave support to the counter-revolutionary movement which emerged in the 1790s, such as that in the Vendée. These reforms reflected the ideas of such men as Voltaire, Rousseau and Montesquieu, who had criticised the system of rule in France in the eighteenth century.

In the meantime, Paris remained very active politically with the growth of hundreds of political clubs such as the Jacobins, which kept ordinary citizens well informed of developments. The capital also continued to be violent, as the new government could not instantly solve France's economic problems. Strikes and riots broke out in 1791 due to high bread prices and this volatile situation continued to drive the Revolution towards more radical measures so as to appease the mob. It was fuelled further when Louis XVI tried to escape from Paris, but his 'Flight to Varennes' was cut short and he was returned to Paris as a prisoner once more in June 1791.

Reactions to Louis' attempt to escape polarised political opinion, with radicals calling for a republic (at the Champ de Mars meeting, for instance) and moderates still hoping for a compromise. The moderates did well to get Louis' agreement to a new constitution in 1791 but the outbreak of war against Austria and Prussia in 1792 led to a renewal of the republican movement and the eventual election of a National Convention headed by Robespierre in September 1792. It was this body that voted to execute King Louis XVI in January 1793 so as to establish the republic more firmly. He was put under the guillotine at 10.22 am in the Place de la Revolution, amid tight security provided by 80,000 troops that patrolled the square and the route to the platform. Once the blade had dropped, the executioner held up the severed head to the crowds so that they had proof of France becoming a republic.

Revolutionary France

By 1793, the effects of the French Revolution had created the characteristics that were to dominate French society for the next twenty years. Amid the cries of 'Liberty, Equality, Fraternity' that summed up the revolutionary ideas there was also extreme and uncontrolled violence; in 1792 for example, the 'September Massacres' of prisoners in Paris gaols occurred which killed up to 1,400 nobles and priests who were suspected of opposing the Revolution. From 1793–5, the Terror claimed another 40,000–50,000 victims. War had broken out against France's neighbours and was to continue almost unabated until 1815, by which time hundreds of thousands had been killed on the battlefields. French society had been irreversibly altered by the rise of new ideals that questioned the authority of the king and undermined the traditional power and stability provided by the nobles and the church. These ideals, however, were often tainted by bloodshed.

To replace the old rulers, Republican France appointed such new political leaders as Robespierre, Roux, Hebert and Danton, whose rapid rise and fall reflected the volatile state of France. What agreement there had been amongst French people in 1793 about how the country was to be organised began to disintegrate as the nation faced the consequences of its own actions: violence, reform and war. People's attitudes polarised into two broad views: those who supported the Revolution and those who opposed it. In the first group could be counted the *sans-culotte(s)*, or urban workers, while the second attracted more support in the countryside. The themes of revolution and counter-revolution were to dominate much of nineteenth-century France as it lurched from one regime to another in 1814, 1815, 1830, 1848, 1852 and 1871, due to revolution and war once again.

During the 1790s, the revolutionary groups' internecine fighting saw more blood spilt as rival factions jockeyed for position. Under the Committee of Public Safety, Hebert was removed, then Robespierre fell and the Thermidorians came to power in 1793–4. On a larger scale, the White Terror of 1793–7 saw a royalist backlash and guerrilla warfare in the Vendée which killed several thousand more people. On many occasions, this was cold-blooded murder; the *noyades*, or drowning of victims on barges that were sunk on the River Loire, killed hundreds, while firing squads and the guillotine were also in common use. The Directory ruled France after a new constitution was drawn up in 1795 and set about restoring law and order as France began to tire of its own excesses and upheaval, and in this it was quite successful.

The reforms that were passed under the Committee of Public Safety centred on a new calendar (dated from 22 September 1792) and a further erosion of the status of the church, so that most church buildings were closed and Notre Dame became, in the madness of the time, a Temple of Reason. Many priests gave up their jobs. The Directory succeeded in stabilising a currency that had become worthless due to inflation, and the taxation system was successfully revamped by Ramel.

In the meantime, France had been at war from 1792. Initially, this was against just Austria and Prussia but it was soon extended to

Britain, Holland and Spain, which were the members of the First Coalition. France became more menacing after issuing the Fraternity Decree, which threatened to export revolution to other countries, and then in 1793 it went on to assert a right to reach its 'natural frontiers'. This meant pushing the French frontiers as far east as the River Rhine, thereby annexing all of the Austrian Netherlands (Belgium) and a substantial part of the United Provinces (Holland). It also meant taking land in the south-east close to the Alps.

France was successful in its war against the First Coalition and expanded in the 1790s, not only into the Low Countries but also into northern Italy. In part, it was helped by the First Coalition's lack of unity, as Russia, Prussia and Austria were more interested in partitioning Poland between them, and by 1798 only Britain was still at war; but France was also successful because the emigration of many (noble) officers had opened up the army to new and talented military leaders, chief amongst whom was Napoleon Bonaparte.

Napoleonic France

On the back of successful military campaigns, Napoleon was able to rise quickly through the army ranks and by 1799 put himself into a position to take political power as well. He first distinguished himself in northern Italy where his small and poorly trained army was transformed into a force that could expel the superior Austrian army. He went on to wage war against Britain from 1798 first by considering an attack across the Channel and then by trying to cut its trading links with the Far East. His invasion of Egypt failed when Nelson destroyed his fleet at the Battle of Aboukir Bay, but Napoleon returned to France in the middle of a political crisis caused by the failure of the Directory to keep order in the provinces. As a result, he took part in a *coup* in November 1799 and was able to convert his position as one of three consuls into emperor by 1804.

Napoleon was a highly efficient administrator who systematised the way that France was governed. This meant that some of the reforms of the Revolution were preserved in law and in French institutions while also strengthening the power of central govern-ment. These two features allowed France to launch more successful wars abroad. A new constitution was devised that allowed the parti-cipation of six million voters but which in practice concentrated power in the hands of the first consul (Napoleon). At first, he held this position temporarily but it became a lifetime appointment from 1802 so that his role began to resemble that of a monarch.

A new legal code, the Code Napoleon, was introduced in 1804 and was followed by criminal and penal codes. These guaranteed certain civil rights, confirmed the abolition of feudalism and ended primogeniture in line with the Revolution's ideals, but workers and women were treated harshly. The population was controlled by an extensive police network and a system of censorship that targeted newspapers in particular. Information was provided in the form of propaganda, typically in the government paper *Le Moniteur*.

In education, élite schools were created to cater for boys who might become army officers or civil servants, and the entire system was supervised by the Imperial University from 1808. Girls were largely neglected, except at a local level in schools that were not formally part of the state system. Regarding religion, Napoleon rejected the anti-church policies of the Revolution and signed the Concordat with the Pope in 1801. This meant the Catholic Church accepted the loss of its lands during the Revolution in return for the French state now paying the wages of the parish priests. The 'Organic Articles' limited the church's independence as far as possible, but the official return of the Mass to France was widely welcomed by ordinary people.

Military reforms were also passed. Perhaps the most important of these pre-dated Napoleon, as the introduction of conscription in 1793 created a nation in arms and the start of warfare conducted by the whole population of a country rather than by a small professional army. The shift meant that armies numbered hundreds of thousands rather than tens of thousands. Napoleon also brought his own military thinking to bear on the army's organisation and from 1800 to 1804 he ensured that the lines of command converged on him alone while allowing his subordinate officers limited scope to make their own decisions during actual fighting. This combination of techniques proved highly successful for a number of years, especially while Napoleon was able to conduct very quick campaigns; however, he became too confident and ambitious and was eventually beaten by a coalition of enemy states.

The Napoleonic Wars at sea

The First Coalition of the 1790s fell apart as its individual members chose to make peace with Napoleon and pursue their own aims. In particular, Russia, Prussia and Austria had designs on Poland, and their final partition of this in 1795 rewarded them with more land. Britain was left to fight on alone until the Second Coalition of 1799, when Russia, Austria and Turkey joined the fray once more. This loose collection of allies, that had not so much formed an alliance as signed a series of individual treaties, was short-lived and collapsed in 1801. Exhausted from lone combat, Britain signed a peace treaty with France in 1802 at Amiens, thereby reaching what turned out to be the mid-point of the wars against France. Neither side had achieved a decisive advantage.

Britain and France returned to fighting in 1803 and Britain soon dominated the sea while France seemed to be impregnable on land. The victory of Nelson over the French and Spanish fleets at Trafalgar in 1805 left Britain in command of the seas; it was made more secure from 1800 when Ireland was annexed as this prevented a hostile force landing there and launching an attack on the British mainland. The British control of the seas also meant that it could harass Napoleon's armies (but no more than that) and seize the colonies of France and its allies such as the Dutch and Danish. In due course, its naval power also enabled Britain to overcome the economic warfare that Napoleon waged from 1806.

Economic warfare was started because Napoleon realised there was little hope of beating Britain's fleet. He tried instead to bankrupt it through the Continental System which allowed Britain to buy goods but not to sell them; in the long run, this would mean the country could not pay its debts and would go bankrupt. In practice, the reverse happened, as continental Europe suffered from the lack of cheap British goods and Napoleon's own army came to rely on boots made in Northampton. The British economy was becoming so strong through industrialisation that it was beginning to defy the basic formula for assessing a country's strength. No longer were land and population size the only influences on power; increasingly, it also rested on the quality of these two features and so a small state such as Britain could 'punch above its weight'. The result was that Napoleon's economic blockade backfired, especially on the undeveloped Russian economy, where, as a result of being cut off from Britain, the volume of trade fell by two-thirds in 1807–8. It was no coincidence that problems here led to Napoleon having to intervene again and this in turn led to the ill-fated 1812 Campaign.

The Napoleonic Wars on land

Napoleon remained victorious on the continent and France soon dominated Europe from the southern tip of Spain to the northern-most reaches of Russia, either through outright conquest or through its system of alliances. The Third Coalition against France disintegrated after Napoleon's decisive defeat of Austria at Austerlitz, or Ulm (1805), Prussia at Jena (1806) and Russia at Friedland, or Eylau (1807), as none of these countries had co-operated with each other. Once again, Britain was left to fight on against France alone. It did so by launching a war in Spain and Portugal which began to bear fruit from 1810 when Wellington won a series of battles against the French commander Massena. The Battle of Salamanca freed Portugal in 1812 and the Battle of Vittoria freed Spain in 1813. Wellington was helped by a guerrilla war fought against the French by the Spanish themselves, and the combined effect was to weaken French power in Europe as it was forced to split its army and fight a war on two fronts.

From 1812, France was not only at war in the Spanish peninsula, it was also fighting Russia in an attempt to force Tsar Alexander I into abiding by the rules of the Continental System. This was the beginning of the end for Napoleon. His armies overreached themselves, as he expected to be able to beat Russia in the summer of 1812 but found instead that the Tsar retreated farther and farther into the heart of Russia, giving up and burning down Moscow in order to wear down Napoleon and deplete his forces. Over the hundreds of miles that Napoleon's troops had marched towards the Russian capital they had been ground down by small skirmishes and a 'scorched earth' policy. This was where the land through which they passed was stripped bare of food or other supplies and it meant Russia avoided the kind of pitched battle that Napoleon liked; the only one of this kind was at Borodino near Moscow, in September 1812.

The overall effect of this was that Napoleon conquered western Russia only to find that his enemy had eluded him by decamping to towns farther east. As Rostopchin, the governor of Moscow said, 'The Emperor of Russia will always be formidable in Moscow, terrible in Kazan and invincible in Tobolsk'. Napoleon decided to return to France almost straight away as his troops could not expect to survive the Russian winter in the remains of Moscow. Of the 600,000 men who left for Russia in the spring of 1812 only 60,000 returned. The Tsar was able to chase the French forces out of Russia and then, crucially, continue to do so beyond the Russian frontier so that Prussia quickly joined in, soon followed by Austria. Britain was keen to have these allies again and its foreign minister, Castlereagh, put together the Fourth Coalition in 1813. After the so-called 'Battle of the Nations' at Leipzig, Napoleon was forced back into France where he found the British forces under Wellington attacking him from the south as well.

This retreat which was forced on Napoleon was thus engineered chiefly by Russia and Britain. It was Russia that was mostly responsible for Napoleon's failure on the mainland; it did not have to pursue him beyond its own frontiers but chose to do so and thereby liberate the rest of central Europe. Britain, for its part, was the only country never to ally with Napoleon and had spent more time at war with France than any other country. Warfare by attrition played its part, but Britain also contributed a small army in Spain and Portugal and effectively paid the wages of foreign states' armies at crucial times by exporting £52 million in gold to France's enemies. Britain's economy took the strain of spending £1,500 million on the war effort which underpinned the diplomatic efforts of its foreign ministers who put together all four coalitions against Napoleon. Above all, Britain was able to dominate the sea by beating Napoleon at the Battle of the Nile (1798) and most importantly at the Battle of Trafalgar (1805) – both of which were won by Nelson.

By 1814, Napoleon felt he had no choice but to abdicate and negotiate the terms of his own retirement as well as the outline peace terms for France itself. There was no way back from his military position, as France was not only surrounded but partially occupied. However, as the four main allies – Russia, Britain, Austria and Prussia – converged on France they began to rival each other for influence and initiative in arranging the post-war settlement and this was to hinder their future progress. Still, France had been clearly beaten and the way was now laid out for a round of negotiations between the allies to reconstruct Europe.

Napoleon's legacy

Most of the allies' efforts had been directed at a military defeat of Napoleon and in the main this was what the Congress of Vienna was also concerned with. The talks that took place there were designed to restore peace to Europe by discouraging France from expanding in future; of course, there could be no guarantees of this, so the peacemakers also tried to ensure that France was reasonably satisfied with the way it was treated. In practice, this meant allowing it a moderate peace treaty. At the same time, the allies took steps to protect themselves further from possible attack, either from France itself or from each other, as they were wise enough to see that their alliance was only likely to be temporary.

The military threat was dealt with, but what was much more difficult to deal with was the penetration of new ideas across Europe which had been spread by the French. There were also problems presented by the effect of the Revolution on France itself and by the unintentional tuition that France gave to Europe's peoples by bringing new ideas through the methods of war and destruction. While historians have differed over the extent to which Europe was affected by the French Revolution and Napoleon, what does seem to be clear is that there was more impact where the French influence lasted longest.

French society had been changed profoundly by the Revolution and wars, and in 1815 the only realistic way forward was a compromise between the practices of the eighteenth-century *ancien régime*, when the king ruled by divine right, and the ideas of the Revolution. The result was to restore the Bourbon monarchy but to tether it to a constitution that granted not only voting rights to an elected assembly for the male élite, but also basic civil rights, such as freedom of religion and of speech, to ordinary people. This was intended to appease the deeply polarised opinions in the French nation: those who were still royalist and counter-revolutionary and those who believed in the Republic or Napoleonic empire and who therefore represented the forces of Revolution one generation further on.

The areas immediately next to France were ruled by France for longest and had most exposure to the new ideas. These included the Low Countries, the Rhineland and north-west Italy. It was the middle classes that were most receptive to liberal ideas, and the French model of representative government framed their political thinking in the years that followed. This was also true of such countries as Spain and Naples that were occupied for a briefer period but which looked for French-style constitutions in the uprisings of 1820, for example. Uneducated peasants and town workers were more resistant to new ideas; for them, the daily concerns of economic life remained more important alongside the traditional church influence. Their experience of French rule was often coloured by forced conscription and this made them understandably hostile. Thus, it was relatively easy for the rulers of Italy and Iberia to restore their eighteenth-century practices, and liberalism seemed to have made little progress.

Farther east, in Germany, there was scope for liberal reforms on a voluntary basis and some of the south German states did grant constitutions temporarily. Most impact was made by the French in Prussia, though, and this was caused not by occupation but by the defeat of Prussia in 1805. In response to losing at the Battle of Jena, Prussia began to modernise its own governmental and economic systems so that its army would be better able to fight in future. Serfdom was abolished, trade guilds were phased out and education was improved. By contrast, Russia and Austria stubbornly refused to bend to the new ideas and stuck to their antiquated systems of government and their backward economic structure. For them, reform was akin to revolution and they resisted it at all levels.

If liberalism made only limited progress, nationalism had still less impact. True, there were popular movements in Germany and Spain to expel the French occupying forces, but they were xenophobic anti-French movements rather than pro-German or pro-Spanish campaigns. What sentiment there was that could be construed as nationalistic, such as the German student groups, was confined to a narrow band of the middle class, and historians such as A.J.P. Taylor have been dismissive even of this. He felt that 'The myth of the German national uprising against Napoleon was . . . fostered by the German intellectuals' (*The Course of German History*, p. 46) and that the 'Battle of the Nations' at Leipzig in 1813 which freed Germany of Napoleon was fought not by nations but by professional armies and conscripts.

In these circumstances, it is not surprising that the allies and peacemakers of 1815 paid little attention to nationalism when they considered Europe's future shape. Liberalism was given more scope in the form of constitutions, but they absolutely opposed the idea of countries being ruled without a hereditary ruling family; republic was synonymous with revolution, and none of them wanted to store up trouble for the future. What was decided at the Congress of Vienna was the direct result of past experience, and this pointed to a conservative but cautiously constructive approach to the new ideas, the penetration of which was not clearly established in 1815 and has not been made certain by the work of historians since.

2

AIMS OF THE GREAT POWERS AT THE CONGRESS OF VIENNA

The war against Napoleon had been fought by the great powers of the Fourth Coalition to ensure their own survival and independence. This remained the priority for each of them, but, as winners, they also hoped for something more. By way of reward, each looked to strengthen their own position by the acquisition of territory either in Europe or colonially, because in 1815 size was everything. Land mass provided the basis of power as it increased population size (and consequently the number of army recruits and tax revenues) as well as providing strategic buffer zones between the heartlands of a state and its potentially hostile neighbours. Since all five great powers operated on this basis and were nervous of each others' future ambitions, there was scope for continued conflict even after the defeat of France; if the post-war settlement was to work, there had to be compromises and an acceptance of rival countries' claims to land. What was agreed in 1815 was the need for a balance of power which rested on the security of all five great powers.

The balance of power

In its simplest terms, the balance of power was a new European order of major states in which no single one of them was able to dominate. What was feared was a repeat of the French domination under Napoleon. However, there was no definite agreement as to what this balance should look like, and what each of the great powers understood by the term was different. To Castlereagh, it was a way of stabilising Europe so that it could return to a condition of what he called 'repose' after the upheaval of war. This was to be a peaceful situation in which each of the mainland powers was satisfied with the settlement and was not likely to dispute it in future. It would leave Britain free to pursue its foreign policy aims elsewhere in the world and not require it to intervene again. The term 'balance of power' had been in use in Britain for some years. The *London Gazette* referred to it as early as 1701 and in 1741 the phrase was first used in Parliament by Sir Robert Walpole; Pitt had outlined what this post-war system might look like in 1804 and Castlereagh drew up a memorandum on very similar lines in 1813. The early evolution of this idea gave him an advantage as the Vienna talks approached, as he already had a set of proposals to put before his allies and this allowed him to take the initiative.

While the British concept of the balance of power sounded disinterested, it was dependent on some territorial changes taking place on the mainland. Britain wanted to feel safe from attack and, during the Napoleonic Wars, had annexed Ireland to deter a French invasion of England via that smaller island. Likewise, it was concerned that an alternative sea route to Britain existed from the huge port of Antwerp which was in Belgium (formerly the Austrian Netherlands). Castlereagh was concerned above all that France did not acquire this territory in any post-war settlement, and was ready to bargain with Britain's colonial conquests if necessary to achieve this aim. As Castlereagh himself said to Lord Aberdeen in November 1813: 'The destruction of that arsenal [Antwerp] is essential to our safety. To leave it in the hands of France is little short of imposing on Great Britain the charge of a perpetual war establishment.' Elsewhere in Europe, his objectives were for a free Spain and Portugal (following Wellington's Peninsular Campaign there) and for a strong central Europe to hedge against the expansion of either France or Russia. To this end, he proposed that Prussia take land in Germany, and Austria take it in Italy so as to preserve a balance.

For Austria, Metternich had devised a very similar idea which he referred to as a 'just equilibrium'. Like Britain, Austria wanted an agreement that would leave itself as safe as possible from attack – Metternich's scheme had less to do with being just than with leaving the Habsburg Empire well defended. His great concern was that the war against France would leave Russia in a position to dominate Europe, and there would be no point in exchanging a French hegemony for a Russian one. He also felt that he had fallen behind in the preliminary negotiations that began to be held between the allies from 1813 onwards because Austria was the last partner to join the Fourth Coalition. He found in the idea of a balance of power a plausible way of limiting Russian power that did not simply look like a means of shoring up Austria's own security *vis-à-vis* Russia. Metternich and Castlereagh were thus able to work together quite closely from 1813 onwards despite certain differences; Castlereagh, for example, was much more flexible about the gains that Prussia might make in Germany than Metternich ever was.

Neither Alexander I for Russia nor Frederick William III for Prussia were keen on the idea of a balance of power at first. Their alliance against France from 1813 onwards gave them an initial advantage in deciding what post-war Europe might look like, as they agreed between themselves on a division of Poland and Saxony that gave Russia the first and Prussia the second of these. The deal was agreed in the Treaty of Kalisch (28 February 1813). While Prussia's gain was bearable, the prospect of Russia annexing the whole of Poland deeply concerned both Britain and Austria; if Russia did so, they felt there would be no balance in Europe at all. Land was the key once more; it conveyed power by furnishing a state with economic and military resources that made it more power-ful. And, in the case of Russia taking Poland, it also represented a huge strategic threat as it could provide a launchpad for an attack on western Europe. This might seem melodramatic, but the experience of seeing French troops in Moscow in 1812 and Russian troops in Paris in 1814 made plain the dangers.

At the start of the talks in Vienna in the autumn of 1814, both Russia and Prussia were holding onto their agreement tenaciously. Prussia was determined to take as much land as possible for itself, including Saxony, so as to become a full great power. Frederick William III was advised well by Hardenberg but the two men were surrounded by their generals who were especially hungry for land and this made Prussian policy more aggressive. Russia's Alexander I foresaw few difficulties in taking Poland: as he pointed out simply, 'there can be no argument with six hundred thousand troops'. But neither leader got all of what they wanted and the Treaty of Kalisch was eventually abandoned. What made this possible and won their acceptance (if not support) of a balance of power was the role that France took.

France was obviously in a weak position in 1814 as the defeated country. Its representative at Vienna was Talleyrand, who readily took to the idea of a balance of power since it would help to preserve France's own position. His aims were modest and amounted to damage limitation, but a balance of power in Europe necessarily involved a relatively strong France to counterbalance the military might of Russia; these two states had the two largest populations at the time and also the two largest armies. Moreover, any balance in Europe might be upset by treating France too harshly and leaving either the population or its ruler aggrieved at the peace treaty and looking for revenge. Talleyrand's grasp of the situation was quick and perceptive. He observed that

> The general equilibrium of Europe cannot be composed of simple elements: it can only be a system of partial equilibrium ... The actual situation admits solely of an equilibrium which is artificial and precarious and which can only last so long as certain large States are animated by a spirit of moderation and justice which will preserve that equilibrium.

Beneath these words was the fear of renewed war; Talleyrand realised that France had to be animated by goodwill and moderation, but so did the other great powers. In the event, it was a temporary alliance of France with Britain and Austria in January 1815 that forced Russia and Prussia, after the threat of war, to give up the Treaty of Kalisch and fall into line with the idea of an overall balance of power for their collective security.

The idea of a 'just equilibrium' was one to which all five great powers subscribed by the end of the Vienna Congress, but with different degrees of support. The balance of power was not to be simply a territorial arrangement; it was, more importantly, a strategic and military balance. It could not be weighed precisely and was not measured or calculated to leave each of the five great powers with an equal share. Nor was it the idea of any one individual who had a clearcut aim for each area of Europe. It was instead a compromise between both the victors and the vanquished which they all considered to be at least satisfactory in protecting their own security.

Table 2.1 Summary of the approximate strengths and weaknesses of the great powers 1815

Country	Population (millions)	Land (000 km^2)	Army	Navy (ships)	Coal (millions of tons)	Iron (millions of tons)
Great Britain	18	315	100,000	235	15	0.4
France	29	550	250,000	71	1	0.25
Austria						
Russia	43	22,000	1,000,000			
Prussia	10		200,000		1	0.4

Great Britain

British foreign policy was conducted by Viscount Castlereagh with the help of three advisers; Viscount Cathcart (ambassador to St Petersburg), Sir Charles Stewart and Lord Clancarty. Castlereagh was foreign secretary from 1812 to 1822 in Lord Liverpool's government and it was this Cabinet rather than King George IV or the Prince Regent to whom he was responsible. While the public and the Cabinet were quite critical of his policies at the time, British historians such as Webster have tended to flatter Castlereagh for his selfless pursuit of aims that were for the benefit of Europe as a whole rather than Britain in particular. But this must be seen within the context of Castlereagh's idea of a balance of power and the securing of Britain's defences first; the refusal to claim any mainland territory was not so much a virtue as a necessity, because it was in Britain's interests to remain free of European commitments (despite a royal link with Hanover) so as to avoid being drawn into future continental wars or alliances. This would leave the country with the opportunity to develop its colonial empire and to enhance its own wealth through overseas trade.

If British security was the overwhelming priority of foreign policy, then the subsidiary aims were all concerned with liberal ideas. Britain pursued economic liberalism (free trade) as a second main objective with political liberalism (constitutions) and humanitarian liberalism (anti-slave trade) as further causes to pursue. By the end of the eighteenth century, Britain was already the world's foremost trading nation and its growing empire provided it with both raw materials for manufacturing and markets for finished goods. This helped to fuel its prodigious industrial expansion, importing for instance an average of 16 million pounds (by weight) of raw cotton in the 1780s rising to 105 million pounds by the 1800s. As a result of a series of wars with France, its main colonial rival, it had won control of India and Canada and, despite losing the thirteen American colonies in 1776, had excluded French influence from the emergent USA. During the wars against France from 1793, Britain had again wrested control of lucrative colonies from France, in the West Indies in particular. British maritime power was enhanced by the war as Nelson's victory at Trafalgar in 1805 had assured British control of the merchant shipping routes. When the Continental System was imposed by Napoleon from 1806, Britain was able to break it by naval attacks on ports such as Copenhagen or by finding new markets, as in the South American republics. By the end of the wars, Britain controlled almost all of France's colonies as well as those of her allies, Holland and Denmark, and was in a position to dictate terms to France. Britain wanted to maximise its ability to profit from world trade. In defiant mood and uncertain of Britain's weight in diplomatic circles, Castlereagh privately asserted the strength of the British position to Cathcart in July 1814 when he said, 'England can be driven out of a Congress: but not out of her maritime rights'. His negotiating position was made stronger by the other great powers' lack of interest in overseas possessions, although he did take care when the time came to ensure that the discussion of such matters was minimised at Vienna.

British foreign policy was conducted with a high moral tone, partly so as to justify it to a critical House of Commons. Splendid soundbites were the stuff of British foreign policy speeches and statements at this time and Castlereagh was ready to provide these in a grandiloquent, if slightly misleading, manner. He explained, for instance, that 'It is not the business of England to collect trophies, but to restore Europe to peaceful habits'. The opportunity for the sub-jects of his majesty to make their fortunes in shipping and trade was seen as an expression of freedom. However, British support of liberal causes extended to two further areas. As the country with the most liberal political system and an unwritten constitution, it was ready to see other countries also adopt constitutions. This was by no means a blanket policy in which constitutional monarchies were to be created in every conceivable case; rather, Castlereagh sought to plant the seeds of liberalism sparingly and only where appropriate. He was conscious of the dangers of sudden political changes, as the French Revolution had demonstrated, and explained at the end of the Congress that

> The danger is that the transition [to liberal politics] may be too sudden to ripen into anything likely to make the world better or happier. We have new constitutions launched in France, Spain, Holland and Sicily. Let us see the results before we encourage further attempts.

Britain was ready to see countries adopt systems of government akin to its own.

Economic and political liberalism were major issues at Vienna, but the last area of British concern was only marginal. Public opinion in Britain had been marshalled by anti-slavery campaigners such as Wilberforce and Clarkson and this meant that Castlereagh was obliged to press for the abolition of the slave trade, i.e., the shipping of captives to colonies, as a step towards the complete abandonment of slavery as a practice. This humanitarian liberalism was viewed with suspicion by the other great powers which saw in it another ploy by Britain to win a commercial advantage since they claimed it had already stocked up on slaves in its colonies. Britain had led the way with the voluntary abandonment of the slave trade in 1807 and had been disappointed not to get some form of agreement on the matter into the First Treaty of Paris which dealt with France before the Congress of Vienna met; consequently, public opinion continued to call for change.

Austria

Klemens von Metternich was responsible for the foreign policy of Austria, on behalf of Emperor Francis I. He had worked in a number of Austrian embassies abroad (Dresden, Berlin and Paris) before being appointed foreign minister in 1809. He was a conservative who belonged to the eighteenth century and who felt that he had been born at the wrong time. Not surprisingly, he was opposed to Napoleon and the ideas of the French Revolution although he had to co-operate with France during the wars so as to defend Austria. Thus, he arranged the marriage of Napoleon and the emperor's daughter Marie-Louise and agreed reluctantly to support the French attack on Russia in 1812. With the defeat of Napoleon, he was faced with the task of furthering Austrian interests at the Congress of Vienna.

However, he was in a difficult position because Austria was not a strong great power. It was threatened by Russia to the east and by France to the west, and its economy and population gave it relatively little support from within. Austria was a composite state of diverse nationalities that were loyal to the emperor but had little else in common; as A.J.P. Taylor observed: 'The Habsburg lands were not bound together either by geography or by nationality' (*The Habsburg Monarchy*, p. 11). The Austrian empire contained Germans, Magyars, Slovaks, Poles, Slovenes, Italians and several other nationalities. Ruling these peoples was a difficult task and the eighteenth-century rulers had centralised government in an attempt to strengthen it; by 1815, 'Administration had taken the place of government', according to Hartig (in Wood's *Europe 1815–1945*). Nor was the emperor optimistic about his empire's condition. He commented to a Russian diplomat that 'My realm resembles a worm-eaten house. If one part is removed one can never tell how much will fall' (*Europe 1815– 1945*). It was for this reason that Austria's foremost foreign policy aim was a just equilibrium.

It also meant that much of Metternich's effort was devoted to minimising the spread of liberal or nationalistic ideas at the peace settlement because either could be destructive of the empire. He opposed the introduction of constitutions for fear that such reforms might lead to revolution or could seep into Austria and undercut the power of Francis. And any growth in national feelings could split the empire into fragments. Much of his diplomacy was focused on preventing other powers achieving their aims rather than creating opportunities for Austria. The balance of power was designed to cancel out the twin threats of Russia and France to the east and west of Austria, and the idea of a strong central Europe was a way of forestalling Prussian expansion into Germany at Austria's expense. To make up for his country's inherent weaknesses, Metternich's diplomacy was very active – and skilled – and during the negotiations at Vienna he allied with Britain (and France, briefly) and then switched to Russia (and Prussia) in the years that followed so as never to be isolated.

Russia

Russian foreign policy was very much the preserve of Tsar Alexander I who was an autocrat in his own country but who nevertheless brought with him to Vienna a large number of advisers from around Europe, each of whom had a special area on which to concentrate. He looked to Czartorski for advice on Poland, Stein and Nesselrode on Germany and turned to the liberals Capo d'Istria and La Harpe for ideas on more general matters. This made it very difficult for the other diplomats to know the mind of the Tsar, as he was apt to change his policies without informing his plenipotentiaries, which could render all their painstaking work useless. Alexander's views were made more complex at this time by his Christian mysticism, emphasised by the arrival of Baroness Krudener to his camp in 1815, which made his intentions harder still to discern.

He was in a very strong position to negotiate with the other diplomats at Vienna because it was the campaign against Russia that had finally defeated Napoleon, and Alexander's massive peasant army of over a million men had overrun Poland and reached Paris by 1814. Annexation of Poland was his priority, and this was going to be difficult to refuse; however, he overestimated the sophistication and ability of the western representatives (which accounted for his large number of advisers) and always suspected some plot or subtle ploy to outmanoeuvre him in the negotiations. As a result, he was hesitant to make any specific demands and delayed making plain his desire for Poland. This was a big mistake, and by the end of the Congress he had actually failed to secure all of Poland.

His long-term aims elsewhere in Europe were no different to those of previous tsars. They had hoped to reach the Mediterranean coast and ideally Constantinople so as to control a warm-water port and open up trade routes, as well as strategic naval links, through the Black Sea. To do this he needed to take land from the Turkish (Ottoman) Empire. During the eighteenth century Catherine the Great in particular had done this after a series of successful wars. From 1806 to 1812 Russia had fought Turkey again and won, but hastily agreed a peace deal at the Treaty of Bucharest so as to prepare for Napoleon's imminent attack. Taken together, the possible acquisition of Polish land and the threat to south-eastern Europe made Russia the most menacing of the great powers once Napoleon had been defeated. While the Russian economy was backward, its labour force was huge and there was a seemingly endless supply of recruits for the army as its land mass reached from the Baltic to the Pacific. Alexander hoped to exploit these resources to make Russia stronger still and had little time in the early stages of the talks for any balance of power.

Prussia

Prussian foreign policy was a simple affair, amounting to little more than a desire to take more land. This was not so much borne of greed as a genuine need to gather territories around itself as a defence against such predatory powers as France and Austria. In the eighteenth century, Prussia was known as 'an army with a state rather than a state with an army', such was the level of militarisation in its society. It was widely perceived as an artificial creation that lacked natural frontiers and could only continue to exist by maintaining a large army on a permanent war footing. King Frederick William III left most of the decision-making to his chancellor, Hardenberg, who was assisted by Humboldt and, not surprisingly, the Prussian army high command. The most prominent general in this body was probably Gneisenau.

Prussia's negotiating position was not a strong one because after its defeat in 1806 at Jena it had played very little part in the wars against

Napoleon. It hoped to have the lands it lost at that time restored to it, and in order to facilitate this had aligned itself with Russia and agreed the Treaty of Kalisch; this was set to give Prussia all of Saxony. It hoped to make gains elsewhere in northern Germany but was reliant on the other powers' decisions. One view that was held unerringly in the Prussian delegation was that France should be punished severely; Webster commented of Hardenberg that, 'Like all Prussians, he expressed always, and without abatement, an undying hatred of France'. It was a measure of the lightweight councils of Prussia that in the final agreements at Vienna, France was treated extremely leniently.

France

Although Louis XVIII had been restored to the throne of France as the new Bourbon king in 1814, it was Charles Talleyrand-Perigord who represented France at the Congress of Vienna. He was a keen supporter of the Bourbons despite previously working for both the French Republic in the 1790s and for Napoleon until 1807. It was he who organised support in Paris for the return of Louis and also lobbied the allies to allow it.

His aims were necessarily limited in scope as France was the defeated country. He hoped only to limit the punishment of France by exploiting any differences of opinion between the four victorious allies. Thus, he hoped to retain the French eastern frontier of the eighteenth-century Bourbons and to minimise any losses either in Europe or abroad. His main concern regarding the other powers was Prussia, which he did not wish to see increase in size as it was a direct threat to France. These aims squared up well with Castlereagh and Metternich's ideas about a future balance of power, and so when the allied split over the Treaty of Kalisch occurred in January 1815 it allowed at least a temporary alliance of France, Britain and Austria against Russia and Prussia. This in turn provided a springboard for France's entry to the important committees that did the work of the congress, so that it had at least some contribution to the talks. The chance to put forward ideas enabled Talleyrand to push for a policy of legitimacy in the reconstruction of European states, a policy on which he was keen since his own ruler had been restored to power by strict hereditary right and which might therefore suggest a restoration of French influence. It also offered a method of removing from power any of the rulers appointed by Napoleon, all of whom Talleyrand detested.

Clearly, the aims of each of the great powers were directed by their own internal strengths and weaknesses as well as by their foreign ministers. The weaknesses in particular had a more profound effect on the formulation of policy than the wars that had just been fought. Certainly, France was to be punished in some way for its aggression and some kind of overall balance was needed – and there was a measure of consensus about this. But the redrawing of Europe's frontiers in 1814–15 was seen primarily in terms of individual advantage by each of the great powers, and the balance of power was what was going to emerge after their bargaining over territories and economic interests had taken place. None of the great powers' ministers was prepared to give away more than was required, and in pushing their own claims to the limit they ensured that the negotiations became intense and fraught. In January 1815, the four victorious powers were threatening war against each other, such was the determination of the diplomats to get their way. Even Britain, with the security of its island status and indifference to mainland territory, and as the country picked out by historians as being most magnanimous in victory, was anxious to preserve its own overseas gains as far as possible. There can be no doubt of the gravity of the meeting or the competition for territorial gain in a settlement that was expected to set the political framework of Europe for much of the nineteenth century.

Pre-Vienna diplomacy

Before considering the territorial settlement that was finally thrashed out at Vienna, it is worth reviewing the preliminary negotiations that were held by the four main allies from 1813, the point at which the defeat of Napoleon first looked likely following his disastrous Russian campaign. These provide an indication of the diplomats' hopes and concerns as the last battles were fought and demonstrate some of the strategies they employed. The meeting that was scheduled for Vienna in the autumn of 1814, and which became the Congress of Vienna, was never intended to take long. It was anticipated that it would merely ratify previous agreements in a matter of weeks and, if necessary, it could tie up any loose ends from earlier talks. In other words, the wartime agreements were meant to be final and binding on the allies. Moreover, any study of the Vienna congress must appreciate that the talks there did not begin in some kind of void, and that previous diplomatic activity had left some powers in stronger positions than others.

The most problematic agreement that was made between any of the allies was the first one, the Treaty of Kalisch. This was signed between Russia and Prussia on 28 February 1813 and sealed an alliance between them to fight on against France. Alexander's willingness to do this had been in some doubt, as it was feared that his only interest was to expel France from Russian soil. The Treaty of Kalisch was therefore an inducement to the Tsar to continue the war. In the terms of the treaty, Russia was to annex all of Poland (except Silesia, which Prussia was to regain) and in return Prussia was to take all of Saxony. This exchange was to their mutual advantage, of course, but it ignored the views of other states. For instance, Austria was set to forfeit all of its possessions from the eighteenth-century Partition of Poland as well as face two much stronger neighbouring states close to its own borders. Britain too was worried that Russia's frontier would extend too far west and, although Britain itself was secure, it feared for the safety of Germany. Russia and Prussia, though, were quite determined to keep to this treaty as they felt that they had taken a serious risk in continuing the fight against Napoleon and that this should be rewarded. Austria, by way of contrast, was slow to declare its hostility to France (it did not do so formally until August 1813) and the penalty it paid was to fall behind in the preliminary agreements.

With Russia and Prussia committed to fighting France in this way, Castlereagh jumped at the chance to sign bilateral agreements with each of them to form the Fourth Coalition in 1813. This was the nucleus of the united front that went on to finally defeat Napoleon. In June 1813, Russia and Prussia were able to draw Austria into their war against France by the Treaty of Reichenbach. This was achieved through a diplomatic sleight of hand for, in order to lure Austria into their group at a time when Metternich was still acting as a nominal ally of Napoleon, they agreed that the future of the Duchy of Warsaw (Poland) was to be decided between themselves, yet Russia and Prussia had also signed the Treaty of Kalisch! Russia and Prussia deliberately kept the terms with Austria vague so that it neither confirmed nor rejected the Treaty of Kalisch. Austria was trapped, but had also been slightly misled. It was a technique that was to store up trouble for the future, but this was the nature of diplomacy at the time and it set a standard for future relations. With the stakes so high, even allies had to be viewed with suspicion. The great powers had been justifiably wary of each other in the past, and it is not surprising that this treaty of 1813 marked the first time all four great powers were at war against France simultaneously, twenty years after the wars against France had begun. The Treaty of Reichenbach still left the allies in a precarious arrangement and one on which Castlereagh in particular was reluctant to rely: he hoped to convert the piecemeal agreements of the Fourth Coalition into a formal treaty of alliance.

The Treaty of Teplitz which soon followed on 9 September 1813 was also purposely vague; this time, the future of Poland was to be decided by an 'amicable' arrangement by Russia Prussia and Austria, but how this was to be achieved was never explained. A further aspect of this treaty was that these three great powers agreed their own territories should be restored after Napoleon's defeat to at least the position that existed in 1805, i.e., before their defeats at Austerlitz, Jena or Eylau. This provides two important lessons. First, that the countries involved were backward-looking when they considered what the reconstructed Europe might look like. Second, they took as a possible benchmark the territorial arrangement of 1805 rather than, for example, 1792. Austria therefore signalled its lack of interest in retaining the Austrian Netherlands (Belgium). It is also interesting to note that in none of these treaties did Britain play any part; this gave Castlereagh (who at this time was not on the continent with his counterparts) a stronger position from which to negotiate at Vienna as a man of integrity who could be trusted. But it also meant that Britain was beginning to fall behind in the race for pledges from other states about the post-war settlement. Remaining in England for so long was a mixed blessing.

Britain fell further behind with its aims in November 1813 soon after the Battle of Leipzig in which Napoleon was expelled from Germany and was forced to cross to the western side of the River Rhine. Metternich devised what became known as the Frankfurt Proposals, which offered generous peace terms to Napoleon since they allowed France to retain its 'natural frontiers'. This meant France could keep all of its conquered lands up to the Rhine, including Belgium. Lord Aberdeen agreed to this on Britain's behalf! This was a serious setback for Britain made by an inexperienced diplomat, since it was an axiom of British policy that Belgium (and specifically Antwerp) should remain outside of French control. Luckily for Britain, Napoleon was slow to accept the offer which was then allowed to lapse, but it prompted Castlereagh to pack his bags for Europe and leave for the allied headquarters in December 1813 so as to direct British policy himself. In the five-way series of talks between France and its adversaries, occurring even while the military balance was shifting, there was a great deal of scope for error and only the wisest statesmen could be relied on.

Castlereagh's efforts were soon rewarded as he made up lost ground quickly through a series of discussions with the other leaders. At Basle, he found that his own ideas about a balance of power matched Metternich's concept of a 'just equilibrium' very closely. At the next meeting, at Langres, it was agreed by the four allies to keep colonies and maritime rights out of the discussions, which was a major achievement for Britain. The other powers assented quite readily and Britain was not obliged to offer anything in return, leaving Caslereagh with a virtually free hand in this area. More importantly, it was agreed that the peace terms to be offered to France in future would be based on its 'ancient limits', i.e., it would not be allowed to keep Belgium and Antwerp. As Castlereagh said in jubilant mood, 'We may now be considered as practically delivered from the embarrassments of the Frankfurt negotiations'.

After a fruitless meeting of the four allies and Napoleon's representative, Caulaincourt, at Chatillon, Castlereagh found himself well placed to put together the formal alliance which he had aimed to do since Reichenbach. Temporary successes for Napoleon panicked the other leaders into signing the Treaty of Chaumont (9 March 1814) which was the last major agreement before the Vienna meeting but the first formal alliance signed by all four great powers. Castlereagh was delighted with its formation and terms and referred to it as 'my treaty'. It was mainly an alliance directed against France, but it also laid out more plainly than at any previous stage what was planned for the post-war settlement.

Under the terms of the Treaty of Chaumont, all four signatories agreed to remain in alliance against France for the next twenty years and not to make any separate peace deals with France. Previous attempts at coalitions or concerted action had often failed because of Napoleon's ability to agree peace terms with individual members, and this had played a large part in his success. Broad agreement was also reached about some areas of Europe. Germany was to become a confederation, while Switzerland was to be independent and Italy was to be composed of separate states. Spain was to be free and ruled by a Bourbon, and Holland was to be enlarged and ruled by the Prince of Orange. The last point was contentious and Castlereagh had to promise large amounts of money and substantial numbers of men for the last campaigns to persuade the other three countries. More controversial still was the future of Poland, yet no mention of it was made in the Treaty of Chaumont. This was probably a further mistake by the Tsar who might have insisted at this point on annexing Poland, and defying anyone to stop him, but the chance passed and any final decision was delayed until Vienna. On a technical level, Article XVI of the Treaty also referred to a 'balance of power' being created in Europe and the countries involved now referred to themselves as the 'great powers'. Here, then, was the making of the Quadruple Alliance.

Table 2.2 Summary of the key meetings and agreements before the Congress of Vienna 1813–14

Date	Agreement	Signatories	Terms
28 Feb. 1813	Treaty of Kalisch	Russia, Prussia	Poland and Saxony to be split between them
27 June 1813	Treaty of Reichenbach	Russia, Prussia, Austria	Austria joined the war against France Poland's fate to be agreed by them
9 Sep. 1813	Treaty of Teplitz	Russia, Prussia, Austria	Poland's fate to be agreed 'amicably' Frontiers based on 1805
9 Nov. 1813	Frankfurt Proposals	None	France to keep its land up to the River Rhine
18 Jan. 1814 to 22 Jan. 1814	Basle Conference	None	Castlereagh and Metternich agreed on a 'balance of power'
24 Jan. 1814 to 28 Jan. 1814	Langres Conference	None	Colonies to be left out of discussions France to be limited to 'ancient limits'
9 Mar. 1814	Treaty of Chaumont	Russia, Prussia, Austria, Britain	All four great powers to remain in alliance against France for twenty years Germany to become a confederation Switzerland to be independent Italy to be composed of separate states Spain to be free and ruled by a Bourbon Holland to be enlarged and ruled by the Prince of Orange A 'balance of power' to be created

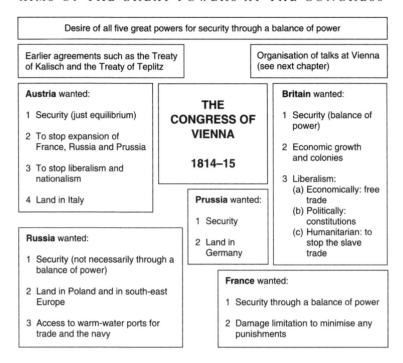

Desire of all five great powers for security through a balance of power

Earlier agreements such as the Treaty of Kalisch and the Treaty of Teplitz	Organisation of talks at Vienna (see next chapter)

Austria wanted:

1 Security (just equilibrium)

2 To stop expansion of France, Russia and Prussia

3 To stop liberalism and nationalism

4 Land in Italy

THE CONGRESS OF VIENNA

1814–15

Britain wanted:

1 Security (balance of power)

2 Economic growth and colonies

3 Liberalism:
   (a) Economically: free trade
   (b) Politically: constitutions
   (c) Humanitarian: to stop the slave trade

Prussia wanted:

1 Security

2 Land in Germany

Russia wanted:

1 Security (not necessarily through a balance of power)

2 Land in Poland and in south-east Europe

3 Access to warm-water ports for trade and the navy

France wanted:

1 Security through a balance of power

2 Damage limitation to minimise any punishments

Figure 2.1 The complex of aims and influences on the Congress of Vienna.

Conclusions

The four great powers that signed the Treaty of Chaumont were reluctant allies, made to co-operate only in extreme need. They came together not to help each other but simply to defeat France after twenty years of largely unsuccessful wars in which the individual pursuit of separate aims had failed. Britain had been France's longest standing enemy and it was this country's foreign secretary who saw most clearly the need to formalise their agreements into a single treaty of alliance. The jealousies remained, though, partly because Napoleon might still have recovered his position and tempted one or more of the signatories to break the treaty, and partly because of the manoeuvring for position in the preceding thirteen months that had left first Austria and then Britain disadvantaged. While Castlereagh had overcome the débâcle of the Frankfurt Proposals, Metternich still had to contend with the Treaty of Kalisch. The Treaty of Chaumont had set out a pattern for redrawing much of Europe but, when the Congress of Vienna convened in October 1814, there was still much to be decided. The security of their own state was the priority for each of the foreign ministers – this, after all was what they had been fighting for – and any support for a balance of power had to be put in this context. As the pursuit of diverse and sometimes contradictory individual aims was never given up, the negotiations were set to be both complex and protracted.

3

THE TERRITORIAL
SETTLEMENT

The territorial settlement of the Congress of Vienna was composed
of three agreements signed between 1814 and 1815. The first element was the first Treaty of Paris (30 May 1814) which was the peace
treaty with France after Napoleon's abdication; the second was the
Final Act of the Congress of Vienna (9 June 1815) which contained
the bulk of the post-war settlement and concluded the months of
negotiations held at Vienna between October 1814 and June 1815;
and the third element was the second Treaty of Paris which revised
the peace terms with France so as to make them slightly harsher after
Napoleon's 'Hundred Days'. The 'Hundred Days' was a three-
month period in 1815 during which Napoleon escaped from exile
on Elba and returned to France, taking back power for himself and
relaunching the war. As a result, the allies punished France more than
before. The Vienna settlement, then, was something that evolved
over more than a year and which was put together in stages

The first Treaty of Paris

The treatment of France was dealt with first because it was the most
urgent matter and followed on naturally from the war. The allied
advance into France culminated in the capitulation of Paris on 31
March 1814 and the entry of Russian troops into the capital.
Napoleon withdrew to Fontainebleau, a short but safe distance
from Paris, and waited to discover his own fate as well as that of
France. The allies had not agreed on any successor – or even if he
should be replaced; Britain had been moving away from letting
Napoleon stay on but was not prepared to remove him by force,
while Austria had initially favoured Marie-Louise his wife (and
daughter of the Austrian emperor) as the best compromise. Russia
preferred the ex-French general and current King of Sweden,

Bernadotte, and was quite hostile to a restoration of the Bourbons. However, it was Alexander who entered Paris ahead of the other allied leaders and it was he who initially took the decision about Napolon's successor by asking Talleyrand for advice. He said: 'We do not wish to settle anything until we have heard your views. You know France, her needs and her desires. Say what we should do, and we shall do it'. As a staunch supporter of the Bourbons, it was Louis XVIII that Talleyrand suggested and this was what was accepted.

As a preliminary to the first Treaty of Paris, the details of Napoleon's future were worked out by Alexander, largely acting alone, and they were compiled in the Treaty of Fontainebleau. In the event, most of what he negotiated with Napoleon was agreed to later by Castlereagh and Metternich, but they were unhappy with his headstrong approach and thought some of the terms were ill-advised. Napoleon was allowed to go into exile on the Mediterranean island of Elba, for instance, just a short distance from the French coast, which was a risk they felt Alexander should not have run. They were proved correct, as he escaped within a matter of months to renew the wars one last time in 1815. His title remained intact, as did that of his wife, Marie–Louise, who became ruler of Parma. Pensions and other details were also settled. Napoleon formally abdicated on 6 April 1814 but was so depressed by even this generous package that he tried to commit suicide by taking the poison he had carried with him on the Russian campaign. To his regret, it failed to work, the chemicals having decayed. By contrast, the Bourbon King Louis XVIII was pleased to enter Paris on 3 May 1814, after Talleyrand had done all he could to drum up popular and political support for him.

Castlereagh and Metternich arrived in Paris on 10 April, ten days after Alexander. Each had been reminded again of the difficulties of maintaining a united front against Napoleon as Alexander had stolen a march on them. The issue of who should become ruler of France had been a question for him alone. There was evidence too of Prussia's King Frederick William III being prepared merely to follow Alexander's lead as, while the talks with Napoleon took place, he excused himself each time so as to go sledging with friends! It was obvious to the allied leaders, though, that Britain was set to become very strong diplomatically because, by having to deal with France first, Britain's concerns would also be dealt with early on and this would almost certainly give it an advantage in subsequent talks. Russia, Prussia and Austria were reluctant to let this happen, but eventually accepted they had no choice, since the alternative meant starting talks on the whole of the rest of the settlement and this was totally impractical.

The first Treaty of Paris was signed on 30 May 1814 and was an extremely lenient peace. Notwithstanding the Prussian generals' desire for revenge, the peacemakers were determined to rehabilitate France into the European state system by arranging a deal that it could accept and later support. The frontiers were reduced to those of 1792 – the ancient limits of France that the Bourbon rulers were familiar with – rather than the natural frontiers associated with Revolutionary France. There were some minor additions for France totalling 150 square miles as tiny foreign enclaves on French soil, such as Avignon, were abolished. France kept a number of its colonies, such as Guadeloupe, as well as its trading rights in India. No indemnity was paid for war damage or costs (the estimated cost to Britain alone was £700 million) and none of the looted art treasures had to be returned. France retained its army and renounced all claims to territories along its borders such as Holland, Belgium, Switzerland, Italy and Germany.

The terms received a mixed reaction. Tsar Alexander was becoming bitter at the lack of progress in resolving the Polish–Saxon question and felt that he was now falling behind. By contrast, Talleyrand was delighted at the French situation, since the peace had not only been lenient but had also left him with a free hand in the next round of negotiations. To him, the treaty was 'as happy as circumstances would allow'. Castlereagh appreciated the advantage of the British position too and remarked, 'I am myself inclined [now] to a liberal line upon subordinate questions, having secured the Continent, the ancient family, and the leading features of our own peace'. Belgium and Antwerp were out of France's reach and British security seemed assured as Holland and Belgium were set to be linked. As the post-war settlement began to emerge, it was plain that there were advantages to those whose concerns were settled first, and in the frenetic diplomatic activity of the preceding months this had not been properly thought through by any of the leading diplomats. It was therefore fortuitous for Britain and France to do so well so early and it was to influence much of their policy-making during the Congress of Vienna proper.

Procedures and course of the Congress of Vienna

In accordance with the agreements made over the summer of 1814, sometimes referred to as the 'London interlude', when most of the plenipotentiaries moved to Britain, the Congress of Vienna was scheduled to begin on 1 October 1814. It was expected to be a quick meeting, but the same problem of Poland and Saxony that had dogged previous discussions was also set to prolong this gathering. Again, little thought had been given to procedural matters, and what organisation there was tended to be arranged on impulse. All of the countries that had fought for or against France, for instance, were invited to attend, and this could have made the talks immensely complex. It was fortunate that a secret agreement between Britain, Russia, Prussia and Austria to keep the key decisions for themselves had been written in to the first Treaty of Paris.

Traditionally, all sovereign states were equal but a hierarchy appeared by the creation of a Directing Committee of Britain, Russia, Prussia and Austria below which were a further three minor states that were a significant part of the allied effort against France: Sweden, Spain and Portugal. In the course of the congress, these took part in the ten subcommittees appointed by the Directing Committee to have special functions or areas to consider. These ranged from quite minor issues, such as the fate of the Duchy of Bouillon, to major territorial areas, such as Germany, Switzerland and Tuscany; they also covered the practical problems of the slave trade, navigation of rivers and the collection of statistics on key areas. This last committee was proposed by Castlereagh and was the first time that the five great powers alone sat on a committee together. It was also significant because it was agreed here that in evaluating the worth or value of a territory the only useful measure was the number of people that it contained; there were no qualitative distinctions in terms of economic development, for example. This underlines the fact that, in 1815, size was everything.

The role of France in the organisation of the meeting was a further

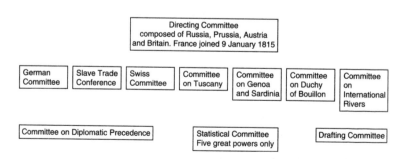

Figure 3.1 Organisation of the Congress of Vienna.

complication. Talleyrand was extremely adept at exploiting the allies' oversights, which included the organisational problems. He wryly observed that, 'Not even the English, whom I thought more methodical than the others, have done any preparatory work on this subject'. In the course of the Congress of Vienna, Talleyrand's impact was threefold. First, he highlighted the great powers' lack of authority in trying to reserve exclusively for themselves the key decisions of the congress (since he was unaware of the secret clause of the first Treaty of Paris) and so he began by championing the smaller states' right to contribute as sovereign states. This intervention meant that the congress never met in full session, with all of the invited parties involved, until the signing of the Final Act in June 1815, because the four victorious great powers created the system of committees.

It was as part of his campaign on behalf of the smaller states that he also made most progress with his idea of legitimacy. Talleyrand tried to foist this idea on the allies as a practical and objective way of restoring peace and order to Europe. But the ploy was double-edged. If it was adopted, it could make France appear to be more important, since Louis XVIII was already a legitimately restored monarch and it would appeal to the lesser states present which were keen to see their own claims – and survival – recognised. In particular, Talleyrand was hoping to see the King of Saxony admitted to the congress because, if legitimacy were applied in his case, it could deny Prussia the right to annex Saxon territory. (Saxony had been excluded because it had remained allied to Napoleon for too long during his final campaign.) This might not only scupper the Treaty of Kalisch, but from France's point of view it would also limit Prussia's growth and thus its threat to France. This was what was at the heart of Talleyrand's policy; by claiming, perfectly reasonably, to support one policy (legitimacy), he was in fact pursuing quite another (French security). Here was an excellent demonstration of the skills of an expert negotiator and diplomat who exploited others' weaknesses even while it was his own country that was the guilty party and cause of the congress. It might also be noted that there was the possibility of a personal vendetta that Talleyrand held against France's former emperor, which meant he wanted the removal of all the rulers appointed by Napoleon. After a disagreement between the two men in 1807, Talleyrand had suffered a personal insult from Napoleon who called him, in terms less polite than this translation, 'a piece of dung in a silk stocking'.

The lack of genuine concern for the lesser states and the absolute precedence given to his own state of France was betrayed by

Talleyrand in his second and third contributions to the congress. Once he had got what he wanted he was ready to forget the needs of the other states, and this was shown when he used the Polish–Saxon question to gain French admission to the Directing Committee. The dispute between Britain and Austria on the one hand and Russia and Prussia on the other concerning this matter has already been placed in the context of the balance of power in which the Treaty of Kalisch would have given Russia all of Poland and Prussia all of Saxony. This was likely to imbalance relations in Europe by Russia reaching too far west and in Germany by Prussia expanding too far south. The split between the four victorious powers had not been resolved despite numerous efforts, and so as late as autumn 1814 it provided Talleyrand with the chance to ally with Britain and Austria and to end French isolation. This is what he worked towards achieving during the lengthy arguments that broke out between the allies in November and December.

Neither pair was prepared to give way, although Prussia vacillated in late October and Britain and Austria nearly won it over to their point of view. By December, however, Prussia was firmly back with Russia again and Hardenberg announced that any alteration to the Treaty of Kalisch might be taken as a cause for war! This was brinkmanship of the most dangerous kind, since it was vital that a united front was kept up against France. The Treaty of Chaumont had been signed in order to maximise the advantages to Britain, Austria, Russia and Prussia of winning the war; now, their internal disagreements were threatening to undo all of that. In desperation, Britain and Austria signed a secret treaty with France on 3 January 1815 which declared their joint hostility to the Treaty of Kalisch. Despite its being secret, the Tsar and King Frederick William III knew the gist of the treaty and Alexander decided, at last, that the Polish lands were not worth the renewal of war. It was only a temporary treaty that France secured, but it was remarkable that, as Talleyrand said, 'France is no longer isolated in Europe'. His delight at French progress was matched by his disdain for his four rivals, whom he described as 'too frightened to fight each other, too stupid to agree'. It was in this way that Talleyrand fulfilled his second aim of ending French isolation, and also his third aim which was to have France included in the Directing Committee (agreed by 9 January 1815). Having achieved this position, he gave up his concern for the lesser states' rights, although he did continue to press for a settlement based on legitimacy.

An agreement was soon reached between the other four great powers as to the future of Poland and Saxony and this paved the way for further progress with other areas under discussion. After January 1815, there were no disagreements to compare with what the Treaty of Kalisch had caused and, as a result, Castlereagh returned to England the following month and was replaced by Wellington. Some problems remained and chief amongst these was the return of Napoleon from Elba for his 'Hundred Days' between March and June 1815. He mustered enough troops tò renew the war against the allies and force a last battle at Waterloo on 18 June 1815. This was won by the allies, having each agreed to maintain an army of 75,000 soldiers mobilised for just such a scenario. Napoleon's return tested the nerve of the allied leaders but they continued with their negotiations in Vienna and by 9 June 1815 the Final Act had been signed.

Table 3.1 Summary of the course of the Congress of Vienna

	Date	*Fourth Coalition/allies*	*France*
1814	January		
	February		
	March	9 Treaty of Chaumont	
	April	23 Armistice signed	
	May	30 First Treaty of Paris	
	June		
	July		
	August		
	September		
	October	1 Congress of Vienna started	
	November		
	December		
1815	January	3 Temporary alliance of Britain, Austria and France	
	February		
	March		1 Napoleon escaped
	April		
	May		
	June	9 Final Act signed	18 Battle of Waterloo
	July		
	August		
	September		
	October		
	November	20 Second Treaty of Paris	
	December		

The social whirl of Vienna

The tension and gravity of the congress proper was thrown into relief by the vast and frivolous social gatherings that Emperor Francis I organised. At the enormous cost of thirty million florins, he entertained the international statesmen, politicians and aristocrats as well as their entourage of families, officials, clerks, ladies in waiting and equerries; and in the milieu there were many uninvited Society hangers-on and ambitious camp followers who were keen to enjoy his hospitality. A 'Festivals Committee' was appointed to arrange the entertainment which found it extremely difficult to keep on coming up with new ideas for the whole nine months. Chief amongst its efforts was the daily evening meal, or banquet, in the Hofburg Palace for forty tables of guests, but the other social activities were wide-ranging. There were balls, galas, medieval tournaments, picnics, drawing room receptions, sleighing expeditions by torchlight through the Viennese forests and hot-air balloon displays. The social whirl was exhausting for those who pursued the entertainment full time; for the diplomats it was often a tiresome distraction.

The Russian delegation distinguished itself by being accused, rather unkindly, of not being properly house trained. Alexander himself was given to flirting with a number of the prettiest ladies at the dances and in so doing crossed Metternich, which soured their relations. Meanwhile, Metternich was busy instructing his servants to collect up any discarded reports or letters from the waste paper baskets of his fellow negotiators so that they could be studied for secret intelligence. Castlereagh took an altogether more austere view; he was a poor dancer and had to take lessons in Vienna, while otherwise seeming content to go window shopping with his wife in the mornings. It was the extravagance of the bulk of these events, however, that helped to attract criticism of the settlement as a whole, as many critics equated the social excesses with foppish and irresponsible decisions about territory.

The territorial settlement: zones

Given the diversity of aims held by the great powers and the degree to which they pursued them, it is perhaps surprising that a balance of power was achieved, but this is what emerged at the end of the nine months of talks. There was no single principle upon which the settlement was based, as at different times and in different cases compromises had to be reached. This was apparent from the preliminary agreements that had already been signed; set against the individual concerns for security there had to be a balance, as stipulated in the Treaty of Chaumont, and while Prussia had wanted a harsh peace treaty imposed on France, the first Treaty of Paris was in fact lenient. Likewise, Russia and Prussia had clung to their Treaty of Kalisch to acquire strategic territory but backed down after intense pressure from Britain and Austria and settled for less. Various ideas can be discerned from the Vienna settlement as it finally appeared, amongst them legitimacy, liberalism, nationalism and territorial aggrandisement, but none of these ever prevailed. What drove the congress was a joint desire of the four victorious great powers to achieve a balance of power that could restore and maintain peace.

Before analysing the extent to which any new ideas appeared in the settlement, it is as well to map out Europe's new frontiers, and to consider how each of the major powers fared, since the Final Act was arranged by them and for them, and not by abstract concepts. To do this, Europe can be usefully divided into three zones – the west, centre and east – to provide an overview. In the west, France was left largely as it had been before; there was no attempt to deprive it of any major area of its territory and in fact it took possession of some small enclaves. But its eastern frontier was sandbagged with a string of medium-sized buffer states that were intended to stop France extending its borders. There was no way that any of them could stand up to France if there was another war, but they would provide time for the other great powers to react either diplomatically or militarily. In the north there was the Kingdom of the Netherlands, composed of Holland and Belgium, and the Prussian Rhineland; in the centre were the larger south German states such as Baden, Württemberg and Bavaria; and to the south were Switzerland and Piedmont. The first of these was a neutral country while the latter, also known as the Kingdom of Sardinia, was enlarged to create a more effective barrier. Together, this series of states was known as the *cordon sanitaire* which might be roughly translated as a neutralised corridor.

In the centre of Europe there was a power vacuum in Germany. By recreating a patchwork of tiny states, none of which had any substantial power, the allies ensured that Germany remained weak. Named the German Confederation, it was not as fragmented as the medieval Holy Roman Empire (made up of over 350 statelets) but was more divided than the Napoleonic Confederation of the Rhine (which had consisted of sixteen states). It helped to keep Austria and Prussia apart, although they did have a common frontier further east.

In Italy, in southern central Europe, there was a second power vacuum of small states which Austria was able to dominate as its sphere of influence. Relatives of the Habsburgs ruled in several of the states while Lombardy and Venetia in the north became sovereign Austrian territory, as much part of the empire as Vienna itself. Germany was more divided but had a national forum for discussion at Frankfurt over which Austria presided, while Italy had no such organisation. Consequently, both areas found it difficult to muster any opposition or independent view of the settlement in the years after 1815 as dissent was stifled by Austria in a deliberate effort to suppress nationalistic feelings.

In eastern Europe, Russia acquired most but not all of Poland, which became known as 'Congress Poland', while Prussia took over half of Saxony in a deal that overcame the worst confrontation for the Congress. The expansion of Russian influence so far west was meant to be tempered by Poland becoming semi-independent with a constitution and ruler of its own, but this turned out to be merely a sham as it was Russia that intervened to quell any unrest when it arose. Russia's other major gain was Finland which it took following a successful war there during the Napoleonic conflicts – and which none of the other great powers could do much to oppose. Also out of reach of the other powers was Britain's acquisition of a great many colonies from France, Holland and Denmark.

These zones explain in simple terms the nature of the balance of power. Each of the winners managed to get some of the key lands that they desired by way of reward for their victory, without being so greedy as to incur the jealousy of each other or the wrath of France or the lesser states. France was barely punished and certainly there was no sense of revenge as it was even spared paying any compensation at this stage. How skilfully balanced the arrangement really was can be debated. In one sense, it was a very mechanical affair, since Russia got a large part of Poland which meant that Prussia had to be pushed farther west to maintain its landmass and Austria therefore picked up the pieces of what was left lying to the south. Alternatively, it could be seen as being carefully constructed so that the two strongest military states of Russia and France balanced each other to east and west, Austria and Prussia cancelled each other out in Germany on a north–south basis and Britain, which could tip the balance one way or the other, preferred to remain aloof and to patrol the sea lanes. Whichever view is the more accurate, this was the nature of the balance of power in 1815.

The territorial settlement: Russia

The balance of power ensured that all of the victorious great powers maintained at least as much territory as they had had in 1805, before the defeats inflicted on them by Napoleon and his redistribution of lands. This did not mean that they regained the same areas of land as they had before, though; while each was keen to keep their core territories, there was the opportunity to rationalise or redirect their landholding by exchanges of territory. The clearest example of this was the effects of the Treaty of Kalisch.

Russia controlled Congress Poland in 1815 which meant that the late eighteenth-century partition of Poland between itself, Prussia and Austria was reinvented but not reproduced exactly. The latter two states gave up most of what had been their Polish possessions but Prussia got Posen and retained the fortress town of Thorn while Austria retook Galicia. This three-way split was reminiscent of the partition of Poland but Russia was now much more the dominant partner. It had been the most controversial area during the congress and, although a compromise was reached, none of the great powers were completely satisfied. Russia had hoped for more and Prussia had wanted more compensation from other lands, while Austria and Britain were uneasy about how far west Russia had come. If there was one way in which a balance of power had not been produced it was over Poland. Castlereagh had deep misgivings about the result but it was Napoleon who expressed most alarm, claiming 'If the Russians succeed in uniting the Poles heartily in a common interest, the whole of Europe ought to dread them . . . They will overrun Europe, and some great change will probably result from it'.

Despite this, Russia was not as successful as it might have been at the congress. It had been in a position to take all of Poland if it had been more assertive or more astute in its diplomacy. It made a big mistake by not including Poland in the Treaty of Chaumont, and then the Tsar was too stubborn during the congress's deliberations to make a quick and clear deal over it because he was always fearful of being caught out by more sophisticated negotiators. His attitude was partly due to his own character, which one commentator described as 'schizophrenic', but which was certainly complicated as he was torn between the traditional tsarist policy of autocracy and expansion and his own mystical Christianity which compelled him towards generosity and liberalism. These features affected Poland in that the area was effectively annexed by Russia in the tsarist manner, but Alexander's conscience was satisfied by granting a constitution

Russia gained:	'Congress Poland'	except Posen, Thorn and Galicia.
	Finland	following the defeat of Sweden and a treaty of 1808
	Bessarabia	following the defeat of Turkey and the Treaty of Bucharest 1812

Figure 3.2 Russia's territorial gains at the Congress of Vienna.

with a nominally independent ruler, his brother Constantine, as king.

Elsewhere, Russia made significant gains which the Congress of Vienna confirmed rather than granted. Finland was annexed with the Aaland Islands following Russia's invasion in 1808 in its war against Sweden. Alexander promised to uphold the rights of the population but in practice never allowed the Finnish Diet to meet and instead styled himself the Grand Duke of Finland with a committee on Finland to advise him that met in St Petersburg. It allowed a relatively liberal regime in the years after 1815. Russia's other major acquisition was Bessarabia from Turkey in 1812 by the terms of the Treaty of Bucharest. This took Russia up to the estuary of the River Danube and closer to Constantinople. It threatened one of the major trade routes of the Austrian Empire which linked it to the sea lanes in the years before railways, although the implications of this were not realised by the Austrians for some time.

The territorial settlement: Austria

If Russia did not do well at the congress, then at least there was some consolation for Alexander in that Austria did worse and, of all the great powers, was left in what turned out to be the weakest position. Metternich worked hard at the Congress of Vienna and was successful in allying with Britain, and temporarily with France, to resist some of the more dangerous moves of Russia and Prussia, but he could not prevent them advancing menacingly towards Austria through Poland and Saxony. His policy was essentially a negative one, perhaps based on damage limitation even more than France's; the positive aspect of his aims was the pursuit of Austrian influence in southern Europe, away from the attention of his rivals. He wisely gave up any claim to the Austrian Netherlands so that Austria could concentrate on becoming an exclusively central European power. He made no attempt to take new German lands and focused on taking land in Italy as compensation instead. The result was still an empire that was being pulled in too many directions at once; it was drawn into Germany in the north, Italy and the Balkans in the south and into Poland in the east. This reflected the view that sheer size lent a country strength, which in 1815 was true, but it left Austria vulnerable to conflicts with Prussia, Russia and Turkey as well as leaving it with the time-bomb of national sentiment that was to break out later in the century in Germany, Hungary and Italy. As industrialisation and national consciousness progressed, size ceased to operate as the key determinant of power.

Germany was made into a confederation in 1815 in line with the Treaty of Chaumont. The allies had no desire to restore the hundreds of tiny states of the Holy Roman Empire that Napoleon had abolished in 1806, but they were not prepared to see his creation, the Confederation of the Rhine, continue either. Castlereagh wanted a strong Germany to act as a bulwark against French expansion, while Metternich wanted it weak so as to prevent it posing any threat to Austria; Frederick William III had a flexible view so long as it involved Prussia getting more land. Set against these views were also the promises of land made by the allies during the war to some of the minor German states in return for supporting the Fourth Coalition, such as the Treaty of Ried (1813) between Austria and Bavaria. There was no single principle that applied here and the final arrangement was put together by the German Committee of the congress which was composed exclusively of German countries – Austria, Prussia, Württemberg, Bavaria and Hanover.

What emerged was a confederation of thirty-eight states (thirty-nine from 1817 when Hesse–Homburg joined) which were independent but united by a Federal Diet based in Frankfurt. It included most of the Kingdom of Prussia but not its eastern provinces, and the bulk of the German areas of the Austrian Empire. It contained the four free cities of Hamburg, Lubeck, Bremen and Frankfurt, duchies such as Holstein and Luxembourg, and kingdoms such as Hanover and Bavaria. Some of these were rewarded with land for their part in the war, such as Bavaria which annexed Wurzburg and the Palatinate of Anspach and Bayreuth (although Austria refused to honour a promise to give it the fortress town of Mainz), and Hanover which obtained East Frisia. Just like the great powers, the small German states were jealous of their independence and anxious to claim land so as to aggrandise their petty kingdoms and (also like their larger neighbours) defend them as best they could.

In no way was the German Confederation the same as 'Germany'. There were many Germans who lived outside the frontier in Poland or Prussia, and there was a range of non-German nationalities who lived inside it such as Italians in the Tyrol and Czechs in Bohemia. Similarly, there were non-German rulers, such as the King of England for Hanover and the King of the Netherlands in Luxembourg. Any German national movement was set to have difficulties reconciling these frontiers with any future state, but satisfying national aspirations was not the intention of the decision-makers here; rather, it was to rationalise the Holy Roman Empire's states in such a way as to fit into an overall European balance. As Webster wrote, 'All this bargaining produced a settlement in Central Europe which almost entirely subordinated considerations of nationality to the idea of balance of power and strategical necessities' (*The Congress of Vienna*, p. 139). And if national concerns were dismissed, so too was Talleyrand's idea of legitimacy since the vast majority of rulers from the defunct Holy Roman Empire were not restored.

Liberalism had more sway in Germany, however, as the Federal Act which laid down the terms of confederation allowed constitutions to be set up. Neither Prussia nor Austria did so but constitutions appeared in Baden and Bavaria in 1818 and in Württemberg in 1819. There was scope for discussion at a national level at the Federal Diet although it was here that Austria was able to assert its hegemony as it held the presidency of the Diet and could thereby direct business. Austria was also supported in the Diet by Prussia for some decades after 1815 and none of the minor states were therefore in a position to oppose their views. The Diet was not democratically elected but made up of the nominated ambassadors of each state. Metternich used it as an instrument of repression to stamp out the stirrings of nationalism when they appeared in the few years after 1815. He galvanised the dukes and princes into concerted opposition to student and university-based groups through censorship and a secret police force which kept extensive files on suspects. These measures were carried through the Diet in the form of the Carlsbad Decrees of 1819 and kept the Confederation quiet for a generation. National sentiment could not be stifled indefinitely though, and problems began to occur in the second half of the century.

In Italy, Austria also dominated. It wanted territory in this peninsula and was in a strong position gain it by clauses set out in the Treaty of Teplitz in 1813 and the first Treaty of Paris in 1814. In the north, Austria regained Lombardy and added to it the former republic of Venetia which together formed a new kingdom directly under Austrian control. These were useful gains as they were wealthy and provided substantial tax revenues as well as access to the sea. They could also defend the route to Vienna should France invade northern Italy as the mighty quadrilateral fortresses stood at the southern end of the Alpine passes to Austria. Next to Lombardy was Piedmont, one of the buffer states of the *cordon sanitaire*, which was intended to slow any French advance in this direction. Piedmont was unusual in Italy as it escaped any form of Austrian influence and was ruled by Victor Emmanuel I, a legitimate and independent monarch.

Much of central Italy was ruled by the relatives of the Austrian royal family, the Habsburgs. The Emperor Francis I, through Metternich, could thus influence their decisions and if necessary support their actions with military force. Parma was ruled by Marie-Louise, Napoleon's second wife, under the terms of the Treaty of Fontainebleau and she was the daughter of Francis I. Modena was ruled Duke Francis IV (a cousin), Tuscany was ruled by Grand Duke Ferdinand III (a brother) and Lucca was ruled by the Bourbon Maria Luisa until reverting to Tuscany in 1847. Austria had a military agreement with Tuscany whereby it could call on its troops if need be. The Papal States were governed by the Pope, Pius VII at this time, who was elected by cardinals to his post and who, as well as leading the world's Catholic believers, also had the rights of a king in Rome, the Patrimony of Saint Peter, the Marches and the Romagna as well as the tiny enclaves of Pontecorvo and Benevento. Austria also had the right to garrison the Legations of Ravenna, Bologna and Ferrara.

The southern half of the peninsula was occupied by the Kingdom of Naples, also known as the Kingdom of the Two Sicilies. It was ruled from Naples by the end of 1815 by Ferdinand I, who was a legitimate monarch, but who only returned to his throne after Napoleon's Hundred Days. This was because the previous incumbent, Murat, had rallied to Napoleon's cause in his last effort against the allies and, being on the losing side, was consequently punished. In the new arrangement, Austria could call on 24,000 troops from Ferdinand in return for which it guaranteed his throne against aggressors.

In all of these small states, the rulers returned to the systems of rule that had existed before Napoleon and his reforming governments. In Piedmont, the efficient French practices were actively rooted out and replaced with the traditional methods of the ruling House of Savoy, while in Naples Ferdinand promised only to alter the constitution he had if Austria consented to this; between them, they greed to abolish it outright. However, Metternich was not able to dominate in Italy as effectively as he did in Germany because there was no equivalent to the Frankfurt Diet. He did try to create something similar to it, but Victor Emmanuel and the Pope both opposed it and blocked the move. Any national assembly in 'Italy' was never going to be one to which 'Italians' could elect representatives because Metternich opposed this, but in any case the population of the peninsula did not conceive of itself as Italian or as belonging to a single country. The backward, uneducated and mostly peasant inhabitants saw themselves as, at best, Neapolitans, Tuscans or Lombards; sometimes their loyalties were to units of organisation closer to home than that, such as the local lord.

There were also sharp divisions within the peninsula. Sicilians did not want to be ruled from the mainland and a strong separatist movement emerged, while the population in the richer northern half looked down on their southern cousins whose land resembled North Africa more than it did northern Italy. Climatic and cultural differences of this kind were preserved by poor internal communications as the country was split east and west by the Apennine mountain range and travel between north and south was limited by the sheer distances involved. There was therefore very little evidence or scope for nationalism in Italy at this time, and Metternich was pleased to comment that 'Italian affairs do not exist'. What unrest there was after 1815 tended to be liberal by nature and the national movement struggled. It was only after 1848 that Austria began to face serious difficulties.

Finally, Austria also took land along the eastern coast of the Adriatic Sea, in Dalmatia, extending down as far as the port of Dubrovnik. The population here was Serb and the land pointed Austria towards Turkey and the Balkans, which was a potential area of conflict with Russia. Turkey had not been invited to the Congress of Vienna and played no part in it, but Metternich saw it as a reliable conservative neighbour and was apt to flatter its Muslim ruler, the Sultan. Again, direct confrontation with Russia in this part of Europe lay well into the future, as did Balkan nationalism, but they added to the way in which Austria was left with a spreadeagled and incoherent empire. Austria contained a multitude of nationalities which were to search for independence later and, far from these peoples lending the empire strength, they became a source of its destruction. Of course, Metternich was not to know the future, but he knew his country's problems and used his diplomatic skills to

Austria gained:	Venetia	the former republic
	Dalmatia	on the east coast of the Adriatic Sea
Austria kept:	Lombardy	
	German lands	
	Galicia	part of Poland
Austria lost:	Austrian	
	Netherlands	voluntarily

Figure 3.3 Austria's territorial gains at the Congress of Vienna.

preserve Austrian influence in Germany, Italy and elsewhere for as long as possible.

The territorial settlement: Prussia

Territorially, Prussia was the most successful of the great powers in 1815 as it accumulated sufficient land to be counted properly as a great power rather than as an upstart German statelet. It had only become a kingdom in 1701 and had annexed land through conquests such as Frederick the Great's War of the Austrian Succession, which secured Silesia, or through the agreement of its larger eastern neighbours which led to the partition of Poland. Prussia's society had also had to be militarised to achieve this. Even so its frontiers remained extremely difficult to defend and this partly explains why the Prussian collapse at Jena in 1806 was so quick when it fought Napoleon. It stuck to its time-worn policy of gathering as much land to itself for protection as possible and the method that Frederick William III used was to stay as closely allied to Russia as possible.

The Vienna settlement gave Prussia some Polish land, Posen and Thorn, as well as about 40 per cent of Saxony's population (which excluded the large town of Leipzig) and 60 per cent of its land area. Castlereagh was responsible for drafting this compromise (thereby overturning the infamous Treaty of Kalisch) which left Prussia with more Polish land than Saxon. As Russia moved westwards, so too did Prussia and this led to its annexation of the east bank of the River Rhine and a large proportion of the Kingdom of Westphalia, the total population of which amounted to some three million people which made up for the loss of as many Poles to the east. All of this was in accordance with the idea of having at least as much land after 1815 as in 1805 and reflected too the work of the statistical committee.

However, the Prussians realised that there were important qualitative differences between the land they had lost and the land they had gained. They regretted losing so many compliant Polish serfs and being put in charge of so many Germans who had been exposed to twenty years of enlightened French rule and who before that had been ruled by Catholic prelates; both of these were out of sympathy with Prussia's severe and Protestant system of rule. Worse still, the Rhineland province was entirely separate from Prussia's other lands and also required Prussia to defend the River Rhine against a possible French attack, since it was one of the buffer states of the *cordon sanitaire*. Prussia had still not solved its problem of having frontiers that were extremely difficult to defend. Such was the dilemma that Prussia found itself in, that A.J.P. Taylor described the situation as being like a practical joke played by the other great powers on the smallest of their number.

In the event, Prussia's position was not so poor. The Rhineland province was transformed over the next few decades into the foremost industrial zone in the world, and its separation from the other lands gave Prussia a strong incentive to bridge the gap and acquire further land. Before doing this, Prussia developed a unified economic system in its own territories which it then extended, to its own advantage, to most of the Confederation. This became the Zollverein (so named from 1834), a free trade zone that unified the forerunner of Germany economically before any political union took place; it served as a template for a new German state as well as demonstrating to a reluctant population the lucrative advantages of forming a single country. While this was the for the future, Prussia also completed a series of land swaps to secure Pomerania on the Baltic coast. It gave East Frisia to Hanover in return for Lauenberg which it then gave to Denmark in return for Pomerania. Here was the work of practical minds that were not constrained by nationalism or ideology to achieve their ends and where the bartering of pieces of land was completed at negotiating tables as readily as if counters were being exchanged at a card table. Altogether, Prussia's population doubled in 1815 from five million to ten million, and this was what it wanted above all.

The territorial settlement: Britain

Great Britain did not want to take any mainland territory for itself and it was content to see a balance of power emerge that resembled

Prussia gained:	Rhineland	as a buffer state
	Posen and Thorn	parts of Poland
	Swedish Pomerania	on the Baltic Sea
	Saxony	60% of its land but only 40% of its people
Prussia lost:	Polish land	to Russia
	East Frisia	to Hanover

Figure 3.4 Prussia's territorial gains at the Congress of Vienna.

the ideas of Pitt's 1805 State Paper and Castlereagh's 1813 memorandum. These had both looked for the independence of Belgium (especially Antwerp) so as to protect the British coastline, and likewise Ireland had been formally annexed in 1801 for this same purpose. Following Wellington's Peninsular Campaign, Britain wanted to see Spain and Portugal free of French influence and this had been agreed at the Treaty of Chaumont. Regarding France, Castlereagh was pleased to see a lenient peace and the return of the Bourbons; he accepted Italy as an area of Austrian influence and was satisfied that central Europe was strengthened by Austrian and Prussian expansion. Russia's annexation of most of Poland was something that worried him, but it had been unavoidable.

Territory was not Britain's only concern. Castlereagh pressed for the abolition of the slave trade but made very little progress apart from extracting vague promises of action from the other great powers. In the event, Britain paid off the remaining countries that practised the trade in a genuine act of compassion and moral leadership; Spain was given £400,000 in return for giving it up by 30 May 1820, and Portugal followed Spain's example by accepting £300,000. The Dutch were not paid in cash, but ended the trade in their colonies in return for keeping most of their colonies in the East Indies, such as Java, which Britain had captured during the war. There were benefits for Britain in being so magnanimous, though; Castlereagh had pointed out: 'I still feel doubts about the acquisition of so many Dutch colonies. I am sure our reputation on the Continent as a feature of strength, power and confidence is of more real value to us than any acquisition thus made'.

Britain could afford to be generous. The continental settlement accorded with its aims very closely; its security was assured and its second main aim of enriching itself was also met by the free trade deals it struck. In Europe, the Committee on International Rivers recommended that they should all be open to shipping and that tolls should not rise unduly. This promised more than it delivered because, in practice, only the River Scheldt was treated in this way; in 1856, the River Danube was opened up by the Treaty of Paris, but the Rhine was not. The Baltic Sea settlement was also favourable to Britain. In short, Denmark was punished for being an ally of Napoleon's by losing Norway to Sweden (which had been promised it during the war). Sweden was then compensated for losing Finland to Russia. For Britain the effect was that the mouth of the Baltic was no longer controlled by a single state (Denmark) and so merchant shipping was more likely to have access to the great ports of Danzig and Riga even in wartime. Napoleon had tried to block off British trade there with the Continental System from 1807, but failed after the British bombardment of Copenhagen.

The biggest gains that Britain made were outside of Europe. It wanted colonies for raw materials or markets, and to provide naval bases from which it could patrol the sea lanes. The naval supremacy that Britain had won after the 1805 Battle of Trafalgar meant that it had captured almost all of France's colonies, as well as those of its allies, Holland and Denmark. In the Caribbean, it kept Tobago and St Lucia from France as well as Trinidad from Spain; and it brought together Demerara, Essequibo and Berbice to form British Guyana in South America. These colonies provided cheap sugar, cotton and coffee which helped to fuel Britain's industrialisation. In Africa, it took Cape Colony from the Dutch as well as the naval base of Mauritius in the Indian Ocean from France. In the Far East, Ceylon (Sri Lanka) was taken from Holland. The sea route to India and the Indies was defended by naval bases on the Cape and Mauritius, while the overland route via the Mediterranean and Near East was protected by acquiring Malta and the Ionian Islands which supported the naval base Britain already had at Gibraltar. Baltic trade was policed from Heligoland, a North Sea island west of Denmark, from which it was taken. The world's shipping routes had not yet been altered by canals either at Suez or Panama, and so Britain built up a global network of bases at key points from which to defend its merchant fleet; this explains the subsequent seizure of the Falklands in 1833, as vessels had to sail around Cape Horn at the tip of South America, and British involvement in Egypt and then the Sudan from the 1870's.

Castlereagh was ready to bargain with the colonies that provided

Britain gained:	Ireland	formally annexed 1801
	Trindad	from Spain for trade
	Tobago	from France for trade
	St Lucia	from France for trade
	Demerara ⎫	
	Essequibo ⎬	from Holland for trade
	Berbice ⎭	
	Cape Colony	from Holland for trade and as a naval base
	Mauritius	from France as a naval base
	Ceylon	from Holland for trade
	Heligoland	from Denmark as a naval base
	Ionian Islands	from Venetia as a naval base
	Malta	from France as a naval base

Figure 3.5 Britain's territorial gains at the Congress of Vienna.

raw materials but not with those housing naval bases. This was despite their high value; in 1815, the French colonies were worth £31 million, the Dutch £39 million and the Danish £5 million. As Britain kept almost everything it held, it paid compensation to Holland for Ceylon (£6 million) and the Cape (£2 million), but all of this money was earmarked for the construction of fortresses along the Dutch (i.e., Belgian) frontier with France. This reinforced the aims Britain had regarding the mainland continent anyway, restricting France behind a *cordon sanitaire*, so the Dutch were employed building defences that Britain wanted in place. British policy was highly successful at Vienna.

The territorial settlement: France

The first Treaty of Paris did not last. It had been agreed at the end of May 1814 when Napoleon had been driven back from Moscow, through Poland and Germany and finally beyond the River Rhine into France from where he abdicated. Before standing down, he had negotiated the Treaty of Fontainebleau which gave him his retirement package, including his exile to Elba, an island close to the French coast and his family's home island of Corsica. But it was too close to France and in March 1815 he escaped to rule France for another three months in the 'Hundred Days'. He rallied many of his troops and officers and fought the Battle of Waterloo, 18 June 1815. The news was not taken well at Vienna, where one observer described the reaction 'as if a thousand candles immediately went out'. They had continued with their work but now took a sterner view of the French who they wrongly thought had all supported his return. The allies decided to treat France more harshly.

The second Treaty of Paris, 20 November 1815, did not substantially alter the territorial settlement despite Prussia (predictably) and the Netherlands calling for vengeance. France's frontiers were cut back to those of 1790 which meant it lost part of the Mont Blanc departement in Savoy to Piedmont. Small strips of land containing fortresses were shaved off the borders in the north-east, specifically Saarlouis and Landau, which became part of the Prussian Rhineland, and Philippeville and Marienbourg, which were integrated into the Netherlands; in other words, the *cordon sanitaire* was tightened. Little has been said of it so far, because its final form was not mapped until this point. The Kingdom of the Netherlands in the north was created by cobbling together Belgium and Holland under King William I and a constitution. These two areas formed an uneasy pairing after 1815 and split apart in 1830. The Vienna diplomats gave precedence to creating a buffer state rather than a coherent society, which was composed of two different cultures: the Dutch-speaking Protestants in the north and the Flemish-or French-speaking Catholics in the south. Farther along the *cordon* was the unwanted Rhenish province that Prussia was granted, and the Swiss Confederation of twenty-two cantons that was made a neutral country in 1815. France had to dismantle the fortress of Huningue as it was a threat to the Swiss town of Basle. Piedmont in the south-east continued to grow like an artichoke, adding layers around its core lands, and it took Nice and Savoy from France as well as the former republic of Genoa. The only other change abroad was that by supporting Napoleon's return, Murat in Naples forfeited his throne and was replaced by the Bourbon Ferdinand I as a legitimate monarch.

France's punishment continued with a 150,000-strong army of occupation imposed on the north-eastern provinces for up to five years (in the event it left after just three) monitored by a Council of Ambassadors. There was an indemnity of 700 million French francs charged by the allies, and a further 240 million accepted as private claims (the figure had originally been 1,200,000 million!). Neither of these financial burdens was too difficult, the fine being paid promptly and the army withdrawing as a result. The biggest economic difficulties

First Treaty of Paris	Second Treaty of Paris
Frontiers of 1792, ancient limits losing Nice and Savoy	Frontiers of 1790, losing frontier fortresses like Saarlouis and Huningue
No indemnity	Indemnity of 700m French francs, plus private claims of 240 million French francs
No army of occupation	Army of occupation for 3–5 years
Kept stolen art treasures	Returned stolen art treasures
Lost colonies to Britain	Lost colonies to Britain
Napoleon exiled to Elba (Treaty of Fontainebleau)	Napoleon exiled to St Helena

Figure 3.6 Differences between the first and second Treaties of Paris 1814–15.

France faced were caused not by the peace but by the war, as sluggish population growth, caused partly by the Revolution's abolition of primogeniture, progressively weakened the potential size of the army and the labour force. The wartime continental system had backfired on France and had left manufacturing industry much weaker. France had few remaining colonies and kept only some isolated trading rights to try to revive itself. To add insult to injury, France had to return the art treasures it had looted during its conquests, such as the Venus of Medici to Florence. Finally, Napoleon was exiled to the remote British outpost of St Helena in the South Atlantic, from which there was no escape. There, he died in 1821.

Despite being harsher than the first Treaty of Paris this second set of terms were not severe. Most of what was changed applied to France's internal affairs and was dealt with quickly. For the rest, the second Treaty fitted in with the larger Vienna settlement very easily and the territorial shifts were, despite the fortifications, little more than symbolic.

Analysis of the territorial settlement

Tracing the presence of liberal, nationalistic or legitimist traits is in some ways a false exercise, because it should be clear by now that these were not the major principles upon which the chief negotiators operated. These ideas were secondary to the balance of power and the individual great powers' aims; Britain supported liberalism mostly for prosperity; France backed legitimacy as a device that could win rights at the negotiating table and root out Napoleon's appointees; and nationalism had no champions except a few radicals and later nineteenth-century historians. The diplomat who was most interested in nationalism was Metternich, and he wanted it suppressed. Nevertheless, a brief review of how far these ideas penetrated the settlement can be instructive in showing what small measure of importance they had and what reactions the settlement has provoked over the years.

By way of summary, liberal sentiments were expressed towards the slave trade but no changes to policy were made, except by the Netherlands in return for its colonies in the East Indies. Free trade got further as Denmark lost control of the entrance to the Baltic, but only one river was made open to all ships and that was the Scheldt. Constitutions meanwhile made rapid but short-lived progress as many states granted them only to abolish them within a year or

Table 3.2 The constitutions of the Vienna settlement

Country	Constitution	Rulers and Details
Denmark	No	Frederick VI
Finland	Yes	Tsar Alexander I did not let the Parliament meet
France	The Charter, 1814	Louis XVIII amended it frequently but it survived beyond the 1830 revolution
Germany	Not till after 1815	Federal Act encouraged constitutions; Bavaria, Baden and Württemberg responded 1818–19
Italy	No, except Naples	See Naples
Naples	Yes (1812)	Ferdinard I abolished it in 1816
Netherlands	Yes	King William did not take it seriously – 'I can rule without ministers'.
Norway	Yes (1814)	Bernadotte granted it
Poland	Yes (1816)	Tsar Alexander I granted it but overruled it in emergencies
Portugal	No	John VI
Spain	Yes (1812)	Ferdinand VII annulled it on his return in 1812
Sweden	Yes	Bernadotte was elected ruler

two. Of the great powers, only Britain had a constitution, but it was not written down as such. By 1815, the situation was as shown in Table 3.2.

Constitutions were always twinned with monarchy. When constitutions were ended, the great powers made no attempt to restore the rights of the people whose freedoms they had usually guaranteed, yet when rulers were deposed by rebellions in 1820–1 or 1830–1 the great powers often restored them. There was a dual standard as the great powers clearly favoured the rulers over the people. Likewise, there was no room in the Vienna settlement for republics, since these were synonymous with revolution. The Venetian and Genoese republics were abolished and absorbed into the lands of monarchs and so was France.

Nationalism was given less credence as it was potentially dangerous to multinational empires – Austria in particular, but also Russia. Germany and Italy did not exist as countries any more than Scandinavia or Iberia, and Poland was at best nominally independent. The number of nationalists in these areas was tiny, and limited to sections of the educated middle class such as students or young army officers. Germany's student groups had been anti-French rather than pro-German during 1813–15, and the efforts of the Italian nationalist Mazzini from 1820 exposed the absolute apathy of most people living in that peninsula. So, although there were more people being ruled by their own nationality in 1815 than in 1789, this was more of a side effect than an intention.

Legitimacy had its symptoms almost everywhere, as rulers were returned to their thrones by strict hereditary right from France to Italy, and from Spain to many parts of Germany. However, there were far more rulers who were not restored, most obviously in Germany which was reduced from over 350 states to just thirty-nine because the great powers wanted Germany to be a power vacuum buttressed by Austria and Prussia; it was plain that the balance of power was more important than legitimacy.

Reactions to the settlement

Reactions to the settlement have varied. The peacemakers themselves were not optimistic for the future of their agreements since there had been so many changes over the previous two decades to rulers and frontiers. This was partly why they endorsed their own previous agreements, such as the Treaty of Chaumont, several times. Their aim of remaining in alliance for twenty years was also a defence against Napoleon returning to power in France. The central plank of the settlement, the balance of power, was inadequate in the eyes of Gentz who felt that the 'agreements between the Great Powers [was] of little value for the preservation of the peace of Europe'.

Informed contemporary opinion was not so much pessimistic as hostile, especially in Britain where the press was relatively free to vent its anger. In 1817 the *Black Dwarf* fumed at the 'accursed principle of legitimacy' and in 1821 *The Declaration of England against the Acts and Projects of the Holy Alliance* lamented, 'Public opinion was disregarded. National feeling was despised, and the expression of it harshly repulsed'. It had anticipated in 1815 that 'the opportunity return to Europe of repairing its many losses, and of regaining the liberties of which its People had for long been deprived'. If some of this criticism was slow to appear, Castlereagh was not spared for so long in the House of Commons, where Whigs such as Whitbread and Mackintosh were critical. In the Cabinet itself Greville 'believed that he was seduced by his vanity [and] that his head was turned by emperors, kings and congresses'.

The defeated countries also felt aggrieved. This was felt most strongly of course in France, where the allies seemed to punish the twice-restored Louis XVIII for the crimes of Napoleon. The second Treaty of Paris was not seen as being lenient, as the allies saw it, but as repressive. French historians have championed this view, and have linked the treaty to the revolutions of 1830 and 1848. In the 1890s Debidour wrote that the allies 'consulted only their own convenience and interest and took no account of the aspirations of the people'. This theme was upheld in the 1950s and 1960s by Ponteil and Droz, but amended slightly by Renouvin, who saw in the Vienna settlement a large measure of continuity rather than reaction, although the results might have been the same.

British and American commentaries on the period have been more flexible and positive, linking the Vienna treaty not to revolutions but to the century of peace that followed it. This was emphasised for Mowat, who was writing in the 1920s, by the difficulties encountered in rebuilding Europe after the First World War in 1918, and then again for Nicolson who wrote in the aftermath of the Second World War. Gulick and Kissinger, as Americans, praised the settlement for its maintenance of stability when their own world was beset by the problems of the cold war. It may be that the years of peace that followed 1815 owed more to rising prosperity brought on by industrialisation or to the post-war Christian revival, or to the states' readiness to resolve disputes by conferences, but it certainly played a part.

Allowing for the bias of the different groups, it seems fair to say that the Congress of Vienna succeeded in tackling the problems that the statesmen saw. War was ended and peace was restored; France was quarantined but not ostracised from the European state system; the winners were rewarded mostly, but not always, with territories that they wanted, and the security of them all was made that much more assured. There was scope for liberalism in constitutions and free trade, and where the former lapsed it was generally the fault of smaller states. The lesser states proved to be more conservative (and more vindictive towards France) than the great powers. Undoubtedly, the statesmen were backward-looking, but they at least cast a glance towards the future.

4

THE CONGRESS SYSTEM

Before the end of 1815, two further alliances were devised that were set to dominate international relations over the coming years. There was the Quadruple Alliance which was signed on 20 November 1815, the same day as the second Treaty of Paris, and there was the Holy Alliance which was set up on 26 September 1815. These two alliances became rivals as each set out a different approach to the future conduct of diplomacy and eventually they played a part in breaking up the good relations of the great powers that they were intended to preserve. The way in which this happened was through a series of congresses which were to be held in a manner similar to the Vienna meeting; despite their doubts about how long the settlement would last – and how close they came to declaring war on each other – the diplomats felt Vienna had been a success overall. As result there were four main congresses that were held between 1818 and 1822 and they have been called the 'congress system'.

Holy Alliance versus Quadruple Alliance

Much discussion has taken place between historians as to the origin of the congress system and whether it lay in the Quadruple Alliance, the Holy Alliance or some other document. In a sense, the debate is sterile because none of the great powers were in practice bound by the terms of the documents they signed and in most cases they deliberately broke the terms. However, an outline of the various agreements involved is useful in showing the evolution of the leading countries' policies after the Congress of Vienna.

The Holy Alliance was the idea of Tsar Alexander I of Russia whose Christian mysticism resurfaced in the desire to create a league of Christian monarchs who could co-operate to keep order, peace and friendly relations between the states of Europe now that a fair settlement of frontiers seemed to have been reached. He was not alone in considering such schemes; Napoleon had toyed with the idea and there were a number of books that suggested ways of pursuing peace in Christendom such as St Pierre's *Projet de Paix Perpetuelle* or Chateaubriand's *Genie du Christianisme*. A more direct influence on the Tsar was Baroness Krudener, a fervent Christian and adviser to him at this time, although he had also mentioned the idea of outlawing war to Pitt as early as 1804. Whatever the case, Alexander drafted the key features of the Holy Alliance and allowed only minor amendments to be included by Metternich.

The Holy Alliance was initially signed by Russia, Prussia and Austria, who declared 'their fixed resolution, both in the administration of their respective States and in their political relations with every other Government, to take for their sole guide the precepts of that Holy Religion, namely, the precepts of Justice, Christian Charity and Peace' so that they would 'remain united by the bonds of a true and indissoluble fraternity'. This was possible because they were 'to consider themselves all as members of one and the same Christian nation'. Every part of the alliance was vague and at best amounted to the statement that its members were part of a Christian brotherhood of monarchs

Reactions to the Holy Alliance were muted as nobody wanted to offend the Tsar. Most of the crowned heads of Europe humoured him and signed up (it was directed at them and not at their governments or states) with just three notable exceptions. The Sultan of Turkey did not sign as he was Muslim; Pope Pius VII did not sign as he was jealous of a Christian initiative that was Russian Orthodox rather than Roman Catholic; and Britain's Prince Regent did not sign. Superficially, this was because he needed the consent of Parliament, but in practice it was because the government was always wary of any open-ended continental commitments. Contemporary comments on the Holy Alliance were disparaging; Castlereagh described it as 'a piece of sublime mysticism and nonsense' while Metternich dismissed it as 'a loud sounding nothing'. The Tsar's naive and bizarre indulgence was out of place in the sophisticated world of international diplomacy and seemed likely to disappear quickly, but it was to be reinvented in 1820 as an instrument of repression to beat off the alternative ideas of the Quadruple Alliance.

The Quadruple Alliance was quite different in character. It was full of practical and specific requirements on which the four victorious great powers agreed, and which they did not invite any other state to join. The second Treaty of Paris was to be upheld and their alliance against France was to be preserved for twenty years. An army of occupation was to remain in France for between three and five years (which also repeated terms in the Treaty of Paris) and Napoleon was never to return to France. Article VI was drawn up by Castlereagh and it was the crucial element in organising the congresses. It said that the 'High Contracting Parties' that is, the four victorious allies, 'have agreed to renew their meetings at fixed periods . . . for the purpose of consulting on their common interests' which was to be for the 'prosperity of the Nations, and for the maintenance of peace in Europe'. It was in keeping with recommendations that Pitt had made during the war, that the eventual victors over Napoleon should 'bind themselves mutually to protect and support each other against any attempt to infringe [their] rights and possessions'. In other words, the Quadruple Alliance was to stay together to protect Europe from future military threats. Article VI was the vaguest part of the document, and intentionally so. Castlereagh could not make his readiness to join with the other great powers any more specific without being criticised and possibly overruled in Cabinet by colleagues who opposed unnecessary mainland involvement. He had seen the advantages of working closely with his counterparts abroad which his fellow ministers had not, and he wanted to continue with them in partnership so as to keep France in check. In order to do so, he had to insert Article VI surreptitiously.

This was the undoing of Castlereagh's aims; because the wording was so vague, there was to be confusion in the following years over when, where and how to call a congress. This gives the lie to the claim that there was any 'system' at all. There were four main congresses, at Aix-la-Chapelle, Troppau, Laibach and Verona, which clearly demonstrates the absence of any headquarters. Nor was there any permanent staff or civil service to support the congresses. The meetings were held at irregular intervals, falling in 1818, 1820, 1821 and 1822, with the middle two congresses almost merging. The first meeting at Aix was called to deal with the remaining problems arising from the treatment of France at Vienna, but there was no such clear reason for any of the remaining three, which, after some hesitation, were convened to consider revolutions. It could also be argued that the absence of key individuals from the congresses made them conferences or one of the other forms of diplomatic meeting; Britain sent only its foreign secretary to one congress, the one at Aix, while France sent only observers to Laibach and Verona. There were no congresses as such after 1822 although attempts were made to hold them. What then is left? The congress system consisted of meetings that were not congresses and which had no system. The phrase seems to be a term of convenience for historians.

The problems encountered from such an early stage in the development of the congress system can in part be traced to its ambiguous origins, but there was a more fundamental reason. The great powers were sovereign states that followed their own policies and they never surrendered their right to pursue their own aims. Thus, in a system that had no means of compulsion, the great powers were free to belong, abstain from or oppose whatever the congresses decided. And this is exactly what happened, as the countries that attended the meetings only went if it was to their advantage to do so. By not joining the system, a country was not isolating itself from the concert of Europe as the 'normal diplomatic channels' of relations between states continued through ambassadors and diplomats working in embassies in foreign states' capitals. The congresses were, then, an extra method of conducting foreign policy which might be considered unnecessary or artificial.

The Congress of Aix-la-Chapelle 1818

The first congress was held from September to November 1818 at Aix-la-Chapelle, or Aachen as it was called in German (it lay in Prussian territory). However, the intervening years had not been devoid of important diplomatic developments, so although Aix was intended to complete the remaining French matters left over from 1815, this was not the only issue. The dominant concern in the courts and counsels of Europe remained the balance of power and in particular the threats to it. For Britain and Austria, this meant Russia. Both of them were concerned about Russia expanding farther westwards and possibly supplanting the domination that France had had under Napoleon. This shared fear ensured that Castlereagh and Metternich continued to work together closely after 1815 and their friendly relationship continued through to 1820. France was not the danger it had been, of course, but the two men also remained wary of its potential aggression. The balance of power was designed to ensure their countries' security, but of the two Metternich felt much more vulnerable as the Austrian Empire was flanked by the two military giants whereas Britain had the protection of the English Channel and its own formidable navy.

Russia had done little to calm their fears. Alexander had not demobilised his army as quickly as the other victorious allies and so his belated suggestion to Britain in the spring of 1816 that there should be a round of general disarmament received a frosty response. Castlereagh proposed instead that Russia disarm unilaterally just as Britain and Austria had done. Likewise, Alexander kept his agents around Europe very active and Castlereagh had to warn the British diplomats abroad not be provoked. Lastly, the Tsar took an interest in helping Spain to end the rebellions that had occurred in its colonies in South America. In the event, Russia simply supplied some old ships to Spain but it had alarmed Castlereagh and appeared to be part of an insidious world policy. The Belgian historian Pirenne has highlighted this by suggesting that Russia was looking to expand on a global scale after 1815 by extending its influence in traditional areas such as the Balkans and into new ones such as North America (since the Russian Empire at this time crossed the Baring Straits). Pirenne took the idea further by seeing the Holy Alliance as a way of countering British maritime power, and the offer to Spain to help assert its strength across the South Atlantic could have facilitated this. Perhaps this is all far fetched, but times were still tense after 1815 and each country looked mostly to its own weaknesses. Thus, Gentz's warning to Metternich was taken seriously in September 1815:

> The relations between the Powers have changed since Vienna. The friendship between Russia and Prussia has chilled considerably; Prussia today stands much closer to us and England becomes more and more estranged from each of us. Conversely, Russia, France and England stand for the moment on the same side.

And this was largely true; Prussia switched its allegiance from Russia to Austria after 1815 as it saw its own defence of vulnerable frontiers was best supported by Austria, which left Russia relatively isolated and keen to befriend France. Britain, in the meantime, was drifting away from continental involvement.

Contacts between the great powers remained in place after Vienna through a number of agreements to supervise the implementation of the 1815 treaty. There were three conferences (or councils) of ambassadors appointed; one in Frankfurt monitored the final territorial arrangements in Germany, a second in London considered the suppression .of the slave trade and a third in Paris had the most important task of enforcing the second Treaty of Paris. It had to oversee the army of occupation and the payment of the indemnity, but also reported on the progress made by Louis XVIII's restoration. These conferences were composed of officials charged with carrying out instructions and they did not take decisions themselves; this was in contrast to the congresses where the statesmen had full authority to make policy.

It was the work of the Paris conference of ambassadors that led to the Congress of Aix-la-Chapelle. This congress met to conclude the work of Vienna and was attended by all of the great powers' rulers or foreign secretaries. The indemnity had been paid off by 1818 and the army of occupation could be withdrawn sooner rather than later, but the Council of Ambassadors did not have the power to authorise this. The congress at Aix did have this power and it allowed the re-entry of France into the concert. This had begun to create friction between the former enemies of France as Russia was keenest to have France join them, while Britain and Austria were much less eager. These attitudes were born of their own selfish interests as Russia was feeling isolated while Britain and France feared for the balance of power, especially if the two strongest military states were to ally. To satisfy all parties, France was accepted back into the concert, but its former enemies renewed the Treaty of Chaumont.

While meeting together, further issues were discussed but with less success. Tsar Alexander wanted to change the Holy Alliance into an *Alliance Solidaire* or universal union of the Vienna signatories that would guarantee the existing rulers their thrones and frontiers. This was to be in conjunction with the granting of liberal constitutions and regular congresses that could direct the use of troops to restore deposed leaders. Castlereagh completely opposed this and threatened to withdraw Britain from European affairs; Metternich was also hostile as he feared the expansion of Russian influence into western Europe. As a result, the scheme was dropped, at least for the time being.

Less important areas of dispute ranged from the suppression of the slave trade, which Castlereagh continued to bash away at without reward, to the policing of the North African coast to stop the plundering of the Barbary pirates. Britain suggested it was given the right to board any vessels suspected of carrying slaves and to stop any pirate ships, but none of the other states were prepared to grant it that much latitude in international waters. Russia was interested in sending troops to South America to crush the Spanish colonies' rebellions but no agreement was reached there either.

Despite these minor problems, the Congress of Aix-la-Chapelle was the most successful of the four. France was integrated into the concert with some degree of consensus, although Richelieu knew who to thank most for this: 'It is owing to the Emperor of Russia, and to his all powerful intervention that we have attained the end that for the last four weeks seemed always to elude us'. Prussia's minimal role was clear, while it was Austria that worked hardest to keep the allies together, for despite the accord there were underlying reasons for a divergence of opinion amongst the great powers and this became obvious in 1820 when the Congress of Troppau met.

The Congress of Troppau 1820

What had not been made clear at the Congress of Vienna was whether the balance of power that was created in 1815 was to be maintained indefinitely or be open to limited change. Was the balance of power to be fixed or fluid? In retrospect, it is plain that the idea of rigidly keeping to the frontiers of 1815 was highly unrealistic, but the Tsar was adamant that he wanted to defend the established order through the Holy Alliance and then the *Alliance Solidaire*. The second option, of allowing piecemeal changes, was open-ended and vague as the scope of any changes allowed could be interpreted in almost any way. The problem created at the time of the Congress of Vienna could not be solved by the subsequent congresses partly because their origins were ambiguous – neither the Holy Alliance nor the Quadruple Alliance gave any mandate for action.

It was only in 1820 that the issue was confronted and it was brought upon the great powers by events outside their control. Rebellions occurred in Spain, Naples and then Portugal that threatened the rulers there and a second congress was called. Alexander was keen to meet again as soon as the Spanish problem arose, but Metternich refused until Naples was affected, since that directly threatened Austria. Clearly, the criteria for holding such a meeting was neither defined nor widely agreed, and this congress drew only Russia, Prussia and Austria. Britain sent Lord Stewart and France sent Caraman and La Ferronay as observers to the gathering that lasted from October to December 1820.

Even before it began, there were signs of problems. Castlereagh issued the famous State Paper of 5 May 1820 outlining Britain's attitude towards European affairs. Foreseeing problems ahead, he emphasised that the original Quadruple Alliance 'was a Union for the re-conquest and liberation of a great proportion of the continent of Europe from the military domination of France . . . it never was, however, intended as a Union for the government of the world, or for the superintendence of the internal affairs of other states.' In other words, Britain was a supporter of a changing or dynamic balance of power in which small adjustments could be made since they would not threaten the peace of Europe. Britain had by no means given up its commitment to a balance of power as it was ready to defend it 'when actual danger menaces the system of Europe', but it was not prepared to continually intervene against minor states.

The three eastern great powers of Russia, Prussia and Austria took the opposite point of view. It took some time for them to reach any agreed procedure for dealing with the uprisings but by 19 November 1820 they released a *Protocol Preliminaire*, which became known as the Troppau Protocol. It asserted the right of these powers to send in armies to restore at the point of a bayonet the existing rulers if they saw fit. This was not quite the language that they themselves used, preferring to couch their claims in diplomatic and semi-religious terms. They explained that:

> States that have undergone a change of government due to revolution cease to be members of the European Alliance . . . If, owing to such situations, immediate danger threatens other states, the Powers bind themselves, by peaceful means, or if need be by arms, to bring back the guilty state into the bosom of the Great Alliance.

All of this was based on a dubious logic, since the announcement appeared to prepare the signatories for the future when in fact it was explicitly directed against the recent past. However, it was very similar in design to the formula devised by Metternich only a year before in the Carlsbad Decrees which empowered intervention in the German Confederation to restore deposed leaders. By another curious shift of meaning, the Troppau Protocol was adopted at this time as the crystallisation of the Holy Alliance, and from this point on the Holy Alliance powers were the three eastern great powers.

The revolutions of 1820–1

So much of the time was taken up in agreeing the protocol that no decisions were taken on any of the three rebellions. In Spain, there was an uprising in Cadiz led by army officers and liberals who rallied around Rafael Riego to force King Ferdinand VII to restore the 1812 constitution. Troops who had been poised to sail to the South American colonies mutinied, too, and with this much strength behind them the rebels went on to make substantial progress over the next two years. The Spanish parliament, the Cortes, centralised administration but did not win over the conservative peasantry because of the former's anti-clerical views. The result was that by late 1822 a civil war was breaking out as the royalist northern provinces tried to overthrow the Cortes.

In Naples the rebellion began on 2 July 1820 and was led by young liberal army officers under General Pepe whose exposure to the ideas of the French Revolution had left them disillusioned by the instant return to repression under Ferdinand I. They too looked for a revival of the constitution so as to counter the elevated powers of the church and the cuts in public spending. The example of the rebellion against another Bourbon ruler in Spain may also have helped to motivate them. By 6 June, Ferdinand had agreed to publish a constitution within a week and having done so he watched the newly elected parliament have to use force to crush the *maestranze* (trade guild) rising in Sicily. In January 1821, he asked to be allowed to plead Naples' cause with the great powers and Pepe agreed; thus, Ferdinand attended the Congress of Laibach.

In Portugal, the political situation was confused by the reigning monarch, King John VI, ruling from Brazil. The royal court had fled there to escape Napoleon's invasion and had not returned; when a rebellion occurred in August 1820, John was reluctant to return and only did so in 1821 so as to deal with the newly formed liberal government. As far as the Holy Alliance was concerned, though, Portuguese affairs were off limits since Britain refused to allow any interference and could insist on this by positioning a fleet of warships either offshore from Portugal or in the broad, deep River Tagus which ran through the capital, Lisbon.

In none of these cases was there any sign of nationalism. The most potent political force of the period was liberalism, and in each example the aim of the rebels was to secure rights for the economic or social élite and to rule in partnership with the existing ruler. The poorer peasant classes were not to be part of this; the rebellions were not democratic and the political nation was confined to the richest tax payers. The early success of the risings was also due to the weakness of the incumbent ruler who could not rely on enough loyal troops to overpower those who were mutinous.

This was also true of the revolt in Piedmont, which began in March 1821, and again a major cause was the severely reactionary policies of the king. Victor Emmanuel I had rooted out many of the enlightened French innovations after 1815 and ended equality before the law as well as free and open trials. Army officers and members of the middle class took control of the fortress of Alessandria and proclaimed a revolutionary government. A few days later, a second army mutiny occurred in Turin. While there were wild shouts in favour of war against Austria and for the 'Kingdom of Italy' most of the energy of the rising was confined to Piedmont's mainland frontiers. Victor Emmanuel I abdicated and in the temporary absence of the heir, Charles Felix, the younger son Charles Albert took over and supported the idea of a constitution. When Charles Felix returned to Piedmont from Modena, his younger brother fled and the new king appealed to Austria for help.

The Congress of Laibach 1821

The third congress was held in Laibach, or Ljubljana, the capital of the Austrian province of Carniola between January and May 1821. It was effectively a continuation of the Troppau meeting, which had adjourned for Christmas and New Year. It was attended by the Holy Alliance powers of Russia, Austria and Prussia whose representatives were Alexander I, Metternich and Bernstorff, respectively, while Britain again sent Lord Stewart as an observer and France sent Caraman, La Ferronay and Blacas in similar fashion. The Holy Alliance had, in the Troppau Protocol, a formula for intervention in minor states' affairs to restore deposed rulers and it was now only a question of time before it was used. Time was something that Metternich used very well. He was assured of Prussian support already because of their mutual defence needs and their co-operation in Germany over the Carlsbad Decrees, but he had to be sure of the support of Tsar Alexander I whose Christian mysticism and liberal aspirations were now wavering.

The British State Paper of 1820 had indicated the problems of continued Anglo-Austrian friendship, and Metternich needed to be careful to win over a new ally in Russia before abandoning Britain to keep Austria within a group of three great powers in a concert of five. He was keen to do this as he recognised Austria's basic weakness and hoped to overcome it by diplomacy and relying on the strength of others. He was helped in this by the Tsar's autocratic tendencies emerging once more when signs of trouble for Russia began to appear. Alexander I had been at his most liberal, in treating France leniently and endorsing its Charter, when such measures were farthest from Russian soil; closer to home, in Poland – where there was also a constitution – Russia could still intervene at will. And in Russia itself, he had allowed an unusually repressive period to be inaugurated under his first minister Arakcheyev. All of this suggested a fair-weather liberal who was obstinately reactionary in the key areas of policy. What began to change Alexander's mind about liberalism abroad were the mildest of political hiccups at home. In March 1819 a Russian agent, Kotzebue, who had been working in Germany was killed. Then, in December 1820, there was a small-scale mutiny in St Petersburg by the Semenovskii Guard which alarmed him much more.

The Tsar caved in. He confessed to Metternich, 'Between 1813 and 1820, seven years have elapsed but they seem to me like a century. Under no circumstances would I do in 1820 what I did in 1812. You [Metternich] have not changed but I. You have nothing to regret but I.' This was what Metternich had wanted to hear, having used the time at Troppau to persuade Alexander of a vast revolutionary conspiracy emanating from Paris. But Metternich had also held back with some decisions, using the time to let panic set into the Tsar's mind, so as to be sure of decisive action when it needed to be taken – as it now had to be. Ferdinand I was there too and urged intervention in Naples not to defend the new constitution as Pepe had supposed but to crush the rebellion. In consequence, 90,000 Hungarian and Croat troops from the Austrian army marched into Italy and easily beat the Neapolitan army at Rieti and on 24 March 1821 they entered Naples itself with olive twigs on their bayonets. On the march back to Austria, the same army went into Piedmont and restored Charles Felix to power. The 1815 settlement was being rigidly enforced.

Technically, this military campaign was the work of the Holy Alliance and not of Austria. Although its troops were used, it was acting on behalf of Russia and Prussia and their protocol. Russia had offered to use its troops in the peninsula but the prospect of Russia sending an army into western Europe was something Metternich was very anxious to avoid. In fact, he had partly delayed using the Austrian troops so as to be sure that while Austria itself was poorly defended the Tsar did not try any aggressive moves – possibly against Austria but more likely against the unresolved rebellion in Spain. Britain was opposed to the whole scheme. It accepted Italy as an area of Austrian influence but thought that a strictly Austrian and not a Holy Alliance army should be used. Castlereagh stressed that, 'The revolution in Naples should be treated as a special rather than as a general question, as an Italian question rather than as a European, and consequently as in the sphere of Austria rather than of the alliance'. Suppression of the revolution was not therefore at issue for Castlereagh and this did nothing to help his reputation in England, where he was caricatured as an arch-reactionary. France was disappointed because it had hoped to ally with Russia, which it wrongly thought was still liberal, so as to secure a constitution in Naples very like its own Charter. This was not so much for liberal reasons as to extend its own influence into the peninsula and begin to rival Austria's domination. No decisions were taken on Spain and, since news of the Greek rebellion only reached the Laibach Congress as it was coming to an end, no decisions were taken on that either.

The Greek revolt and the Eastern Question

The rebellion that broke out in Greece in April 1821 was different in nature to the uprisings in Italy and Iberia. It was not so much a liberal as a nationalist revolt begun by Alexander Ypsilanti in Greek merchant colonies on the Black Sea coast, but it spread to the Morea and subsequently the Aegean where Greek domination of the islands and seaways gave them a genuine chance of success against their Turkish overlords. The Greek leaders wanted to break away from the Turkish Empire to become an independent state, which was Christian and free from the persecution of the Muslim Sultan Mahmud II. It was on these grounds, of being brother Orthodox Christians, that Ypsilanti appealed to Tsar Alexander for help.

The Turkish Empire had not been affected by any of the territorial changes wrought by the Congress of Vienna but the stability of the empire was a grave threat to the entire settlement. The Greek rebellion had the potential to undermine the Turkish Empire if it served as an example to other disaffected areas in the Balkans or North Africa to rise up against the Sultan; or, more plausibly, it could stir one or more of the great powers to intervene against Turkey and the ensuing war could leave Turkey teetering on the brink of collapse. It was widely accepted that, as 'the sick man of Europe', Turkey was in terminal decline, but the consequences of it breaking up were unimaginable. 'The complications which may ensue in the East defy all calculation', warned Metternich. At worst, there was a fear of the Greek revolt opening up the entire Eastern Question and possibly drawing the great powers into general war with each other. This fear was not misplaced, as the next major war between Europe's great powers, the First World War, was triggered by problems in the Balkan states.

Each of the great powers had some stake in the Eastern Question, but they were united by a common attitude which has been summed up by the phrase 'everyone hates the Turks'. While this seems glib, it was true that as Christian states they despised the barbarity of the Muslim Turks towards their Orthodox Christian subjects. Massacres occurred periodically which inflamed European opinion and it was against this background that Russia claimed a right to protect all Christian subjects in the Turkish Empire from the 1774 Treaty of Kutchuk–Kainardji. The same treaty had given Russia substantial areas of hitherto Turkish land following its defeat in war by Catherine II of Russia, and in particular it gave her empire its first foothold on the Black Sea coast. From there, Russian influence had expanded either through further war (such as the 1806–12 war ending with the 1812 Treaty of Bucharest) or through commerce as the Greek merchants flew the Russian flag on their ships and duly prospered in the late eighteenth and early nineteenth centuries. The overall effect of these advances was to make Russia the largest single threat to the Turkish Empire and in a position to attack and win territory almost at will, since the Turkish army and navy were both weak. Russia wanted the land to improve its population size and thus its recruitment and revenues but the prize above all was to take Constantinople which would give Russia unlimited access to the Mediterranean. This, of course, was something that Russia had in mind even at Vienna but which the other great powers opposed just as strongly.

Austria too was looking for territory in the Balkan area of European Turkey and in 1815 had acquired the Dalmatian coast. Prussia only shared in the general concerns of the great powers about the Eastern Question, while France had begun its involvement in the Levant as recently as 1798, when Napoleon landed his troops in Egypt. He did this to launch an economic war against Britain by cutting off its overland trade route to India and the East. This attempt failed after the Battle of Aboukir Bay, but French interest remained as it complemented their ambitions in the western Mediterranean. Britain for its part was determined to protect its lucrative trade with the Far East and was concerned to prop up the Turkish Empire for as long as possible. Far from invading parts of it, like the French, Britain wanted to preserve Turkey as the best way to resist Russian expansion.

The Congress of Verona 1822

Against this background, a further congress was called and held at Verona in Austrian-controlled Lombardy between October and December 1822. It was the last of the four meetings of the system and was dominated by Metternich and Alexander. France sent Montmorency and Chateaubriand as observers and Britain sent Wellington in the same role. Castlereagh had intended to join this congress because he considered the Eastern Question to be of sufficient weight to threaten Europe's balance, and in particular he was worried about the dangers of Russian intervention. Metternich felt the same way, and the two men met up at Hanover in 1821 to discuss the matter at a conference. Britain and Austria seemed to be drawing closer together again as they were also concerned about Russia or France invading Spain. However, in August 1822 Castlereagh committed suicide and was replaced by his arch-rival Canning, which temporarily threw British policy into some confusion. Wellington therefore travelled to Verona while Canning familiarised himself with policies in London. In the meantime, Metternich also saw the Tsar at a private meeting, sometimes dubbed the 'Vienna conference', just before the congress proper to try to reach an early understanding.

Verona failed to take any definite action. It was as much as they could achieve to make a joint declaration that the Greek revolt was a 'rash and criminal enterprise' and for Alexander's desire to intervene to be kept in check by Metternich. Regarding other matters, a Protest Note was sent to Madrid warning the Cortes of the great powers' concern at the nascent civil war in northern Spain. France was considering intervention on its own which angered Britain and especially Wellington as he had liberated Spain from French rule only ten years before, and this alarmed Metternich as he feared that the French would then try to set up a constitutional monarchy under a system very like their own. In the meantime, delay tried the patience of the Tsar more and more. In the face of tense international relations, the Verona congress merely kept up a facade of unity (through carefully worded statements) when in practice the great powers' views had diverged. It seemed less and less likely that the 1815 settlement was going to survive intact for the first decade.

The importance of the congresses

This was as far as the congress system reached. After Verona, there were no formal gatherings of the great powers to compare with Aix or even Troppau and Laibach. There was an attempt, at St Petersburg in 1825 (to deal with the Greek rebellion), but it did not attract all of the great powers and their failure to reach decisions highlighted the

Table 4.1 Timeline of congresses, conferences and their causes 1815–25

	Congresses and conferences	Revolutions	Other events
1815	VIENNA (till June) Paris, London, Frankfurt		
1816			
1817			
1818	AIX-LA-CHAPELLE (Sep.–Nov.)		
1819			Mar. Murder of Kotzebue Sep. Carlsbad Decrees
1820	TROPPAU (Oct.–Dec.)	Jan. Spain July Naples Aug. Portugal	May State Paper Oct. Troppau Protocol Dec. St Petersburg Mutiny
1821	LAIBACH (Jan.–May) Hanover (Oct.)	Mar. Piedmont Apr. Greece	
1822	Vienna (Oct.) VERONA (Oct.–Dec.)		
1823			
1824			
1825	ST PETERSBURG?		

various states' independent attitudes. This was at the heart of the problems of the 'congress system'.

So far, the account of the congresses has followed a conventional line by outlining the decisions taken at the meetings and explaining the subsequent actions; however, there is an alternative view that there is only a superficial link between the meetings and the action taken. In fact, it can be argued that the congresses achieved nothing in themselves. At best, they speeded up diplomatic activity but also, by artificially forcing the great powers together, the congresses drove the wartime allies apart. This was quite the opposite of their stated aims in either the Quadruple Alliance or the Holy Alliance.

The Congress of Aix-la-Chapelle was the most successful as it completed the work of Vienna. But this first meeting relied for its success on the work of the Council of Ambassadors in Paris which had done all of the groundwork in supervising the French restoration, repayment of the indemnity and military occupation of the north-eastern provinces. The assembled dignatories at Aix did not need to decide anything new as the army could be withdrawn, under the Vienna terms, after just three years. The treatment of France was thus reduced to a ceremonial occasion as the victorious allies rubber-stamped the work of their underlings. When other issues arose, there was immediate disagreement. From the *Alliance Solidaire* to the Barbary pirates and from the slave trade to the colonies of South America, the great powers could not agree, and the exchanges between Britain and France became quite acrimonious. None of these issues had been prepared in the same way as the treatment of France had been.

The suppression of the Italian revolts in Naples and Piedmont were not the work of Laibach and Verona. Italy was accepted as an area of Austrian influence by all of the great powers, even Britain, and so Austria was quite within its jurisdiction when it sent an army there. It is perhaps dangerous to rely on counter-factual techniques in the analysis of history, but there is overwhelming evidence that Austria was going to intervene anyway. From the start, Metternich was determined to see the rebellions crushed as they were so close to Austria and it was their proximity that made him agree to the Laibach congress at all; he had previously rejected the idea when the Tsar suggested a meeting over Spain. He relied on the congress only because of his anxiety over Austria's weakness. In January 1820, he only had 20,000 troops available to send into Italy while the Tsar had amassed 100,000 very near to the Austrian border. The Russian army was a threat to Vienna and Metternich wanted to be confident that when he gave the order to use his smaller force it would be both safe and decisive. He was fairly certain of Prussian support following the Carlsbad Decrees but still sent out a communique to all of the German courts to galvanise their opposition to unrest. By preparing the way so carefully, he managed to provoke Castlereagh into an uncharacteristically panicked message of support for intervention, declaring, 'If Austria thinks fit to set her shoulders to the wheel there be little doubt of her competence to overrun the kingdom of Naples and dissolve the rebel army'. If Castlereagh was becoming impatient, Tsar Alexander I was approaching exasperation at Metternich's delay and of course lent him overwhelming support for action in Italy. Only France remained aloof from Metternich's web of diplomacy and in this way the Austrian army of the Holy Alliance eventually entered Italy in 1821 to do on behalf of the alliance what Austria most wanted for itself.

Much of Metternich's work was done at the congresses, which might point to their importance. It is true that they provided a forum for discussion which accelerated diplomatic developments, but in this they simply made the suppression of revolution in Italy come sooner rather than later, for the 'normal diplomatic channels' of ambassadors and couriers could have achieved the same effect. What the congresses also did was to drive the great powers apart earlier than might have otherwise happened. By trying to reach agreement, and confronting each other with complex international problems, the great powers were compelled to set out their views on European security, the balance of power and revolts in a way that had been avoided (or overlooked) at Vienna. The clash of opinions expressed in the State Paper and the Troppau Protocol in 1820 split Europe along east–west lines with the autocratic Holy Alliance countries opposing the liberal monarchies of Britain and France. Foreseeing the problem of a congress dealing with revolts, Castlereagh wrote the State Paper five months before the Troppau congress in an attempt to clarify Britain's position; the Troppau Protocol was a reply and a repudiation of it which took the whole of a congress to draft.

What then is left? The re-entry of France to the concert and the crushing of the Italian revolutions were dealt with at the congresses but achieved nothing distinctive or new in themselves as they did not alter any country's policy. They speeded up the polarisation of Europe into two groups by 1820 and aggravated rather than eased international relations by trying to bring separate sovereign states together. Moreover, the areas discussed at the congresses were amongst the simplest – France and Italy – whereas the most difficult international problems were left untouched by the congresses. Thus, the rebellion and subsequent civil war in Spain was dealt with later not by the Holy Alliance but by France on its own, while the Greek revolt was also resolved later by a joint military force from France, Britain and Russia. Very little seems to be left of what part the congresses played. Their importance has been exaggerated because of the convenient turning-points they seem to present and partly because historians have found in them a forerunner of the twentieth century's attempts to form international organisations such as the League of Nations and United Nations. It is a mistake to see the congresses in isolation from other forms of diplomatic activity that ran simultaneously with the congresses such as the Councils of Ambassadors, conferences and normal diplomatic channels of communication. All of these methods were employed simultaneously with the congresses as the great powers pursued their aims. These activities allowed relationships to develop between the major states that were counter to the direction the congresses seemed to be taking them. The rift between Britain and Austria after 1820 exemplified by the State Paper and Troppau Protocol was by no means absolute as they continued to share a fear of Russian and French military strength. The interests of each state were long term and could not be overturned by quick-fix congresses.

From Castlereagh to Canning

Much has been made of the reasons for the failure of the congress system. Its inherent weaknesses were clear; it had no headquarters, no army or civil service, no procedures for calling meetings and no founding document. However, none of these were insurmountable problems and if the great powers had been in agreement on key issues action could have been taken more quickly. A great deal of attention has also been given to the personal relationships between the men who met at Vienna and how their friendships helped to sustain the post-war co-operation. This view has its limitations. It was propagated in part by Metternich, whose diplomatic banter flattered his listeners in order to keep them friendly but who could be equally caustic when he chose. The most obvious case of this happening was when Britain's policy appeared to change after the death of Castlereagh and his replacement with Canning. Metternich described Castlereagh as 'my other self' but called Canning a 'malevolent meteor, this scourge of the world, a revolution in himself'. However, the role of individuals and their friendships was minimal and so was the turnover of personnel.

The death of Castlereagh in 1822 did not alter British policy. Canning adopted Castlereagh's guidelines for the Congress of Verona which were also agreed by Wellington, that is, to try to prevent France intervening in Spain and Russia from doing the same in Greece. The direction in which Britain had been moving, in recognising the South American rebel colonies' belligerent status, was maintained by Canning subsequently accepting their full independence. And in Portugal, Castlereagh had contemplated sending a fleet to Lisbon which Canning duly did in 1826. What set the two men apart was their personalities and style of working. Castlereagh was reserved, modest and from an aristocratic background while Canning was flamboyant, brash and had no title.

The former suffered from a bad press since he had to defend the government's repressive home policies as leader of the House of

Commons and was seen as conniving with continental autocrats in Vienna. His own poor speaking style was commented on by Greville, who thought it was 'prolix, monotonous and never eloquent', but it hardly matched the attacks he suffered from poets. Shelley damned him by penning a couplet 'I met murder on the way/He had a mask like Castlereagh', and Byron was earthy in his criticism, saying 'Posterity will ne'er survey/A nobler grave than this/Here lie the bones of Castlereagh/Stop, traveller and ****!' By contrast, Canning mastered his own public relations with memorable sayings to stir the hearts of British patriots. 'Every country for itself and God help us all', he declared and, more cautiously: 'For Alliance read England, and you have the clue to my policy'. Some of his claims were mere rhetoric, such as 'I resolved that if France had Spain, it should not be Spain with the Indies; I called the New World into existence to redress the balance of the Old', but his recognition of the South American colonies in this way was made into a triumph. The clash of personalities led to a duel between Castlereagh and Canning in 1809, and professionally they personified the two alternative approaches to British foreign policy that ran through the nineteenth century. Castlereagh was followed by Aberdeen and Gladstone in trying to co-operate with foreign states while Canning, Palmerston and Disraeli were more competitive and defiant in their style. None of them, however, changed Britain's basic aims abroad which remained fixed on security, trade and liberal causes, in that order.

There was otherwise a measure of continuity in the personnel who were responsible for foreign policy, as Metternich remained at the helm for Austria until 1848 and Frederick William maintained his steadfast support of Austria until his death in 1840. French foreign ministers changed more frequently, but Louis XVIII and Charles X shared the same aims and tried to find allies and reassert French power after the isolation and defeat of 1815. The most significant change in leadership occurred in Russia in 1825 when Alexander I died and was succeeded by Nicholas I. The new Tsar was keen to become involved in the Greek revolt and rejected Metternich's overtures to remain out of the conflict. The personal relationship that Metternich had nurtured with Alexander had perhaps played a part in holding Russia back, but he played upon the mind of a Tsar who was by nature hesitant and complex. However, this occurred outside of the congress system and the period after 1822 was marked by a period of flux in international relations as the great powers realigned themselves to deal with the problems of Spain and Greece.

Spain and Greece

The rebellion in Spain was a threat to the Vienna settlement in so far as it might topple the king, Ferdinand VII, and permanently change the system of rule established there but there was no immediate danger of any frontiers changing. In April 1823, a French force of 100,000 men under the command of the Duke of Angouleme crossed the Pyrenees and entered Spain. Little resistance was encountered and the north was soon pacified and Ferdinand restored to power, whereupon he resumed the repressive methods he had used before. Alexander was pleased to see the rebellion ended in any way at all, but Britain and Austria were both hostile as it allowed French influence to be extended just a few years after its defeat and Metternich was worried that France might foster liberal ideas in the country. What is surprising is that, having distanced itself from the Holy Alliance, France was ready to intervene in the affairs of another state. Its reasons for doing so were twofold. First, it wanted to restore a legitimate monarch and to show that it was anti-revolutionary. Second, it was also keen to demonstrate its strength once more in an area that it considered to be part of its sphere of influence. While these messages might have been reassuring, Britain and Austria were unnerved by the rapid recovery of French military prowess. There was little they could do, though, as France was a sovereign state and a great power that could not be changed from its course except by force. This was the nature of European diplomacy then, as before.

Greece was a more complicated issue. Tsar Alexander I of Russia had been on the verge of intervening on the Greeks' behalf several times. While he was opposed to rebellions, he saw the chance to attack Turkey which might provide more gains for Russia and he hated the butchering of Orthodox Christians that was taking place (although he was less concerned about the atrocities they themselves committed against the Muslims). In 1822, 25,000 Christians were massacred on the island of Chios and 47,000 were sold into slavery. This news also shocked the British public, which was influenced already by the departure of about a thousand Romantics, such as Byron, travelling to Greece to join the rebellion. British policy-makers faced a dilemma; they wanted to shore up the Turkish Empire so as to keep the area stable, but were unsure of how best to do it. Britain tried to avoid intervention, but its own ruling class was sympathetic to the Greek cause having been educated on the history and literature of classical civilisations. Trade was being affected, too, and there was a danger of British banks suffering losses. With both European security and British trade at stake, Britain was tempted to intervene.

The international situation changed almost overnight with the death of Alexander I and the accession of Nicholas I in 1825. Alexander had been struggling to find a policy and in 1825 had organised the St Petersburg conference to discuss the question with the other great powers but with no results. The Nesslerode Circular of August marked a hardening of policy with its assertion that 'Russia will follow her own views exclusively and will be governed by her own interests'. When Nicholas became Tsar, he decided to take this a stage further and to help the Greeks; this was despite Russia's commitment to the Holy Alliance and in response Britain offered to join in any campaign in the Aegean so as to moderate Russian policy. This, of course, was in breach of Britain's own State Paper. In April 1826, the St Petersburg Protocol was signed between Britain and Russia which proposed the creation of a virtually autonomous Greek state and France joined them in the Treaty of London in July. All of this by-passed Metternich and his efforts at mediation. 'The Continental alliance, on which our peace and prosperity rests, has ceased to exist', he said, and it was true that the east–west split of 1820 was in abeyance at least on this issue as the individual states pursued their own interests regardless of their previous agreements.

The joint land and sea operation against Turkey was swift and effective when it came. After the failure to secure an armistice between the Turks and Greeks, an allied fleet anchored off Navarino Bay while Russian ground forces marched south. In October 1827, after a misunderstanding by Vice-Admiral Codrington who was in overall command of the fleet, the allied ships attacked Turkey's and destroyed them. Sixty-one Turkish vessels were sunk, leaving just twenty. A land war also broke out 1828–9 which Russia won, and in the Treaty of Adrianople in September 1829 Turkey was forced to accept the semi-independent state of Greece as well as minor concessions to Russia. Turkey was seriously weakened by the loss of its fleet but was otherwise still intact and Russia was content to have a neighbour that posed no threat to it rather than try to take more land. Britain was pleased to see Greece break away and Turkey survive.

Conclusions

The history of international relations from 1815 to 1830 shows the failures of the congress system, if such existed, rather than its successes. It was an additional tier of diplomacy to try to build on the successes of the Congress of Vienna, but it never had the same importance as the threat of France was receding. It was, as Castlereagh said, the danger of French domination that had sealed the Fourth Coalition and Treaty of Chaumont; co-operation in the war against France had been achieved with some difficulty and there was in practice little chance of five great powers agreeing on pan-European problems such as rebellions in the period of peace that followed. The different outcomes of the revolts demonstrated the great powers' pursuit of separate aims and their readiness to work with each other on specific problems when the need arose. Thus, the Holy Alliance provided a general policy statement for Russia, Prussia and Austria but not one that was binding and Tsar Nicholas broke it in helping the Greeks. Likewise, the State Paper was qualified by Britain's defence of its own interests in Greece. Power rested with states that could enforce their will and so Italy was invaded as it was part of Austria's sphere of influence, Spain was occupied temporarily by France as it dominated the western Mediterranean and Portugal escaped because British sea power could protect it. The application of this kind of power was a stark rebuff to the niceties and subtleties of drawing-room diplomacy and set the pattern for the decades that followed. The continuation of the Congress of Vienna settlement was to depend on the great powers, not on their peoples or the minor states of Europe. This, after all, was what made the great powers great.

5

BREAKDOWN OF THE SETTLEMENT 1830–1914

By 1830, there had been no changes to the European frontiers as laid down at the Congress of Vienna. Although Greece had emerged as a new state, the Turkish Empire from which it had broken away had been excluded from the settlement. By 1848, the maps had still not changed significantly; the *cordon sanitaire* had been altered only to allow the separation of Belgium from the Kingdom of the Netherlands, and in eastern Europe Austria had annexed the previously free city of Krakow.

Forces for change and continuity 1830–48

This apparently stable situation had not been achieved without strenuous efforts by the three eastern powers, and by Austria in particular, which had organised the Holy Alliance to try to police Europe and the Carlsbad Decrees to stifle change in Germany in particular. Uprisings in Italy were crushed in 1821 and again in 1831 through the intervention of Austrian troops, and the minor unrest in Germany which took the form of two festivals, at Wartburg (1817) and Hambach (1832), led to increased repression organised from Vienna via Frankfurt.

Most of the uprisings in Europe from 1815 to 1848 were liberal rather than nationalist in character as largely middle-class men, typically serving in the army, protested against the harshness of their rulers in Naples, Piedmont, Portugal and Spain on a local basis. The protestors wanted reform, not revolution, and hoped above all for a constitution to guarantee the rights of the social and political elite. All of the rebellions in western Europe failed; the same fate met the Polish uprising (1831) in eastern Europe, which was nationalistic and crushed quite easily by Russia.

National sentiment was more successful in the west: separatist movements rose up in Belgium and Greece, but they needed the support of the great powers to achieve independence. Britain was instrumental in each case. It compelled France to leave Belgian soil twice through Palmerston's 'gunboat diplomacy' in the early 1830s so as to prevent France encroaching into its *cordon sanitaire*. It therefore continued to defend its own security by monitoring the potential threat of a naval attack from the Low Countries. It also joined with France and Russia to help Greece throw off its oppressive Turkish overlords.

The 1815 settlement was threatened not only by liberal and national movements, but also by the military danger of France. It had tried in vain to take land from Belgium in the 1830s and had attempted to extend its influence into Italy by encouraging a French-style constitution in Naples in 1820. A French army invaded Spain in April 1823 but only to restore King Ferdinand to power rather than to find any territorial advantage for itself. Nevertheless, along each of its frontiers, France was looking to reassert itself after 1815. In the event, the only area of French expansion was in the sand dunes of North Africa, where Algeria was developed as a colony from 1829.

The threats to the Vienna settlement were, then, the twin problems that had been identified in 1815; the military danger of French expansion and the scope for liberal or national unrest from foreign populations following their occupation by French armies. The treatment of these two threats was a victory for neither the fixed frontiers approach of the Holy Alliance outlined in the Troppau Protocol nor for the more flexible idea of a dynamic equilibrium put forward by Britain in the State Paper. By 1848, a territorial balance of power remained in Europe which was very similar to that of 1815 and which reflected the work of both camps.

A changing balance in Europe 1848–56

The year 1848 was dominated by revolutions that broke out all over Europe. Beginning in Paris in February 1848, they spread to Germany, Italy and Austria and continued to cause problems for the great powers until 1850. None of them were successful except in France where the monarchy of Louis-Philippe was toppled and replaced by the Second Republic, shortly to be followed by the Second Empire of Napoleon III. The revolutions elsewhere might better be named rebellions, since a revolution that fails is no revolution at all. And the reason for their failure was simply Russia.

The risings in 1848 were more nationalist than those of 1820–1 or 1830–1, and it was the hope of many political activists in Hungary, Italy and Germany that they could unite their countries as separate states while also meeting the liberals' demands for constitutions. The various rebellions lasted as long as they did (which in most cases was still only a few months) because they happened simultaneously and stretched the resources of the great powers that were under attack. Thus, Austria was most vulnerable and suffered most as it faced Hungarian separatists, a war in Italy against rebel forces that united behind Piedmont and German nationalists in Frankfurt who were helped for a time by Prussia.

Like Britain, Russia experienced no revolution in 1848, but unlike Britain, it played an active part in suppressing them. Tsar Nicholas I had no sympathy with any kind of rebellion and he cared little that national or liberal ideals lay behind the unrest in Europe. So concerned was he about the threat they posed that he crushed the rising in Hungary on Austria's behalf so that the government in Vienna could concentrate its efforts on Austria first of all, and then its hinterlands of Italy and Germany. This chain reaction meant that Prussia, which had faced an uprising in Berlin in March 1848, was discouraged from courting the revolutionary movement for too long. Its king, Frederick William IV, aspired to lead a united Germany dominated by Prussia and in the heady 'March Days' of 1848 wrapped himself in the nationalists' flag of red, black and gold while riding through the streets of his capital. This gave the national cause a huge boost.

However, the assistance that Russia gave to Austria meant that Frederick William IV quickly back-tracked in 1849. He refused the crown of Germany offered to him by the revolutionary National Assembly that had convened in Frankfurt and in 1850 he accepted the Treaty of Olmutz which restored the German Confederation of 1815. He did this because Austria still had Russia's support. Against the combined strength of Austria and Russia, there was little prospect of him leading a united Germany. The saviour of Austria in 1848–9 was undoubtedly Russia and for this it expected, not unreasonably, Austria's friendship and support in the future.

'We shall amaze the world with our ingratitude', said Schwarzenberg, Austria's leader in 1850. And so they did. Despite being indebted to Russia, Austria refused to help it when called upon to do so in the Crimean War just four years later. Russia was left to fight on its own territory without a single ally against the combined forces of Britain and France (and eventually of Piedmont too) and consequently lost a war for the first time since the early eighteenth century. Austria watched uneasily from a position of neutrality but seemed, by 1856, to be edging towards joining the war against Russia. The reaction of the Tsars, both Nicholas and his successor Alexander II, was unbridled anger. The very country whose existence they had ensured only a few years before had completely abandoned them.

It was the diplomatic outfall from war that ended the Vienna settlement, not the efforts of the 1848 revolutionaries. Russia had been beaten and was forced to accept peace terms in Paris that it bitterly resented. The Black Sea clauses of the Treaty of Paris that concluded the Crimean War meant the Black Sea was demilitarised and the Straits of the Dardanelles that gave entry to the Mediterranean Sea were closed to Russian warships. These terms were imposed on Russia and it wanted them changed; while it turned to internal reforms in the 1860s, it waited for a chance to end the Black Sea clauses, possibly by allowing another country (or countries) to change their European frontiers in a reciprocal deal. This reversed Russia's previously reactionary policies. Whereas it had been conservative and fought to uphold the established order in Europe before 1856, it was now ready to see changes. This shift in attitude also meant that it jettisoned Austria as an ally.

The desertion of Austria by Russia was the beginning of the end for the Austrian Empire. Austria was left isolated after 1856 and it failed to secure any allies until 1866 – by which time it was much too late. Austrian policy under Metternich had carefully cultivated diplomatic links with other countries, whether it was Britain in 1815–20 or the Holy Alliance powers of Russia and Prussia after 1820, so as to avoid diplomatic isolation. He had understood how vulnerable Austria was and had tried to conceal it or compensate for it by using his skill as a diplomat. If Austria was weak in the period 1815–48, it was even more so in the 1850s because it had not only lost its main ally but it also suffered very heavily economically. Despite not fighting in the Crimea, it had kept its army mobilised and this had depleted its resources; in 1857, it suffered a major financial crisis.

Moreover, the wider diplomatic balance in Europe was turning against Austria. The new French leader, Napoleon III, was keen to see changes in Europe (avowedly based on nationalism) and he had been joined by Russia. Britain, as ever, remained relatively aloof and anyway was not averse to changes in Europe, which meant that Prussia became the only possible conservative friend Austria could find. But Prussia had revealed its ambitions in 1848–9 when Frederick William IV had placed himself at the head of German nationalism and had tried to wrest the leadership of Germany from Austria. In a Europe composed of five great powers, two favoured change (France and Russia) one was aloof (Britain) and two – for the time being – wanted stability (Austria and Prussia). It seemed that it only needed an initiative from Prussia to tip the balance in favour of change. As Bismarck, the leader of Prussia in the 1860s, wryly observed, 'It all began with the Crimean War'.

The end of the Vienna settlement: Italy and Germany

However, the first substantial changes to the Vienna settlement were effected not by Bismarck's Prussia but by the policies of Cavour, the leader of Piedmont. He launched an aggressive war against Austria in 1859 and won, which meant Austria was expelled from Lombardy in northern Italy. This created an enlarged north Italian kingdom which quickly led to the creation of a new country: Italy. Bismarck engineered a war against Austria in 1866 which left Prussia in control of northern Germany and he then mounted a war against France in 1870–1 which led to the Prussian domination of southern Germany, as well. He had looked only for the aggrandisement of Prussia but in the process created another new country: Germany. Both men exploited the weakness of Austria and the realignment of the European diplomatic balance after the Crimean War to achieve their aims.

Cavour realised the weak position that Austria was in and had learnt as much as anyone from the lessons of the failed uprisings in 1848. At that time, the nationalist forces of Italy had united behind Piedmont in a war against Austria and had been beaten. In other words, when the weakest of the great powers was at its weakest, it had fended off the military threat of Piedmont, the strongest of the Italian states when it was at its strongest. Cavour rightly concluded that there was no way that Piedmont could dislodge Austria from the Italian peninsula without outside help. Help was needed from a great power and that great power had to be France.

As leader of France, Napoleon III proclaimed his support of nationalism which he saw as the most powerful movement of the age. In order to make France more powerful, he decided to ally himself with it and in 1858 he turned his attention to Piedmont as he felt that Italian nationalism deserved his support. This, however, betrayed a limited perception of nationalism as he only wanted to

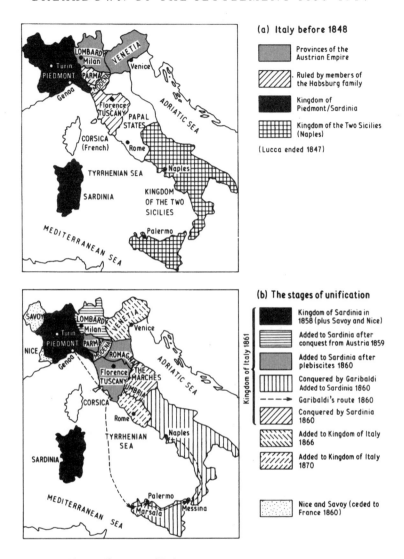

Map 5.1 The unification of Italy.

unite Italians in the northern part of the peninsula while the Kingdom of Naples and the Papal States were out of bounds. To this end, he met with Cavour at Plombières and they agreed on a scheme to attack Austria so as to 'free Italy to the Adriatic', i.e., to force it out of Lombardy and Venetia. The war that followed was fought largely by France, and at the battles of Magenta and Solferino Austria was roundly beaten. It retreated to the four huge fortresses of the Quadrilateral that guarded the Alpine passes to Austria and dug in. This deterred France from pursuing the war any further, but signalled Austria's weakness. It had, for instance, had to fight alone.

While the war was under way, Cavour sent Piedmontese troops south into the central Italian states of Parma, Modena and Tuscany and took control of these areas from their Habsburg rulers, while also marching into the Papal State of the Romagna. Austrian influence was being systematically rooted out. What he was aiming for, and what he briefly achieved in March 1860, was an enlarged Piedmont. Unexpectedly, the south of Italy was also brought into the nascent state of Italy by the heroic guerrilla war fought by Garibaldi, who conquered Sicily and Naples in 1860 with the help of volunteers who seemed drawn to his charismatic personality as much as to the nationalist cause. Nevertheless, it was through force of arms that both the northern and southern parts of Italy were taken over by these men and then cobbled together into a single, unified (if not entirely united) state called Italy. By the end of 1860, only Venetia, Rome and the Austrian Tyrol remained outside the frontiers of modern Italy. Unification, though, had not been a process entirely of integration as France's reward for helping Piedmont was to annex Nice and Savoy; it did this in 1860 and so breached the 1815 *cordon sanitaire* for the first time.

In Germany, a similar pattern emerged. The creation of Germany in 1870 was not a matter of the German people coming together and uniting by consent; far from it. Prussia took over large parts of the German Confederation and asserted effective control over the states that remained intact. It was led from 1862 by Bismarck whose aggressive policies led to a succession of wars. His ruthless approach to policy-making was quickly demonstrated by his solution to an internal dispute between the Prussian parliament and the king, William I, concerning the modernisation of the army. He chose simply to ignore the parliament and to collect the taxes that it had refused to grant regardless of its protests. With the army stronger because of the reforms that began from 1862, he was in a better position to direct Prussian policy.

His first steps were faltering, although his own memoirs would have us believe otherwise. When Poland rose up in rebellion against Russia, he sent General Alvensleben to Moscow to offer help to the Tsar to crush the rebellion in the Russian and Prussian areas of Poland. For this, he was condemned in diplomatic circles and felt compelled to deny his intention. However, the message that Tsar

Alexander II received from Bismarck's first move was that Prussia was friendly to Russia and wanted to co-operate. This, of course, was in marked contrast to Austria, which was still isolated. From this position, initially he worked with Austria in north Germany where they occupied the duchies of Schleswig and Holstein so as to prevent their annexation by the King of Denmark. Bismarck managed to annex Schleswig and then use Holstein as a pretext for declaring war on Austria in 1866.

The Austro-Prussian War was fought not just by these two great powers, but by members of the German Confederation (with Austria), all of which were very weak, and by Italy (with Prussia), which meant that the Austrian forces had to be split in half to fight a war on two fronts. Austria was thus largely isolated, as it had been since 1856, while Prussia had been very active in preparing for a possible war by securing allies (even if they did not fight, such as Russia) and ensuring the neutrality of others (such as France, which had been duped into believing it would receive land on the Rhine if it kept out of the war). The result of the conflict was a surprise to contemporaries, who felt that the two sides were quite evenly matched; instead, Prussia won the 'Seven Weeks War' quickly after beating the main Austrian force at Sadowa (also known as Konniggratz) in July 1866. By the peace treaty signed at Prague, Austria lost no German land, but Prussia annexed Holstein, Hanover, Nassau and Frankfurt and had control over the newly formed North German Confederation which was all of the old German Confederation (of 1815) except for the four south German states of Bavaria, Baden, Württemberg and Hesse, all of them south of the River Main.

Bismarck had observed that, 'The position of Prussia in Germany will be decided not by its liberalism but by its power', and he was now demonstrating exactly that. He used its military strength and economic resources, mustered through the Zollverein free trade zone and the rapid industrialisation of the 1850s, to inflict a form of unity on a Germany that resisted it. He had contempt for the liberal ideas of the 1848 revolutionaries and went on 'not through speeches and majority decisions are the great decisions of the day decided – that was the mistake of 1848–9 – but by blood and iron'. This *Realpolitik* was the brutal exercise of power, but it was not without restraint. Bismarck did not want to simply accumulate more and more land because he did not want to dilute the identity of Prussia; instead, he wanted to build up Prussia's strength gradually so that new lands could be "Prussified."

This took place in the North German Confederation after 1866 and no new schemes of aggrandisement were begun until 1870. Then, Bismarck took advantage of an incident that was not of his own making to make France appear aggressive and warlike. By threatening to put a German prince on the throne of Spain (and thereby surround France), he provoked France into making the issue a matter of honour and then into declaring war. He has been accused of being a warmonger, and even the king commented that, 'he smells of blood, and can only be employed when the bayonet rules'. But this is unfair. Bismarck used war as an instrument of policy to achieve a limited and specific end. In 1870, he wanted a war or major foreign success because he knew from the experience of 1866 that it would rouse German nationalism and only this seemed to provide sufficient force to lift the south German states out of their parochial independence. By winning a war against France, he knew he could extend the North German Confederation farther south.

This was duly achieved in the Franco-Prussian War of 1870–1 after an impressive Prussian attack that pinned down many French troops in the fortress of Metz and defeated the remainder at the Battle of Sedan, 1 September 1870. The subsequent annexation of the eastern French provinces of Alsace and Lorraine, that was to leave France embittered and keen for revenge until the First World War, was not something that Bismarck had wanted. The Prussian army generals were responsible for this piece of military trophy-gathering, lacking as they did the understanding and statesmanship of Bismarck. The war led to the declaration of the German Empire in 1871, but this was in practice an enlarged Prussia, just as Italy was an expanded Piedmont.

By 1870, the Vienna settlement was at an end. True, some of its main features remained unchanged, such as the frontiers of Britain and Russia; but central Europe was significantly different as two new states had emerged as the loose collections of states in the geographical areas of Italy and Germany had disappeared. Moreover, the political boundaries reflected a real shift in the balance of power as Germany stood as the most potent military presence in Europe. From the late 1860s, each great power took steps to improve its own armed forces, usually in line with the Prussian example, to take some account of the new state of affairs. The ancient axiom that power rested primarily on land and population no longer held true. While it still had some significance, what was also needed by the 1860s was an industrialised economy that could produce modern guns in large numbers and which had a transport system, based on railways, that could move troops and equipment quickly and

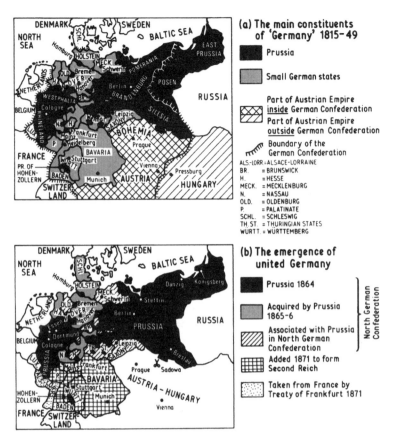

Map 5.2 The unification of Germany.

efficiently. This had been demonstrated as early as 1859 when France sent troops to Piedmont, and in the 1860s by Prussia which mobilised more quickly than either Austria or France. The quality of its troops was also better as its education system worked more effectively. Size was no longer as important; well-trained armies and well-managed economies were also needed.

It was ironic that the Vienna settlement, which had been made possible by the military campaigns against Napoleon, was in turn brought to an end by warfare. And, set against the standards of 1815, it was the work of two ambitious upstart states, Piedmont and Prussia, that was responsible for the settlement's demise. They demonstrated the impact that small, well-run states could have on larger ageing neighbours.

Table 5.1 Changes to the Vienna settlement 1815–1914

Date	Land	From	To
1839	Belgium	Netherlands	Independence
1846	Krakow	Free city	Austria
1860	Lombardy	Austria	Piedmont/Italy
1860	Parma, Modena Tuscany, Romagna Naples	Independence	Piedmont/Italy
1860	Nice and Savoy	Piedmont	France
1866	Schleswig/Holstein Hanover, Frankfurt Nassau	Independent	Prussia
1866	German Confederation	Independent	North German Confederation or four independent south German states
1866	Venetia	Austria	Italy
1870	Rome	Independent	Italy
1870	Bavaria, Baden Hesse, Württemberg	Independent	German Empire (with North German Confederation
1908	Bosnia/Herzegovina	Semi-independent	Austria

Epilogue

There were some further changes to the European frontiers after 1870, chiefly in the Balkans. However, since the Turkish Empire had fallen outside of the Vienna settlement they did not alter it as such; rather, Austria extended its frontiers in 1908 by annexing Bosnia–Herzegovina after previously operating a protectorate over it. While there were a series of Balkan wars in south-east Europe, frontiers did not substantially change until the end of the Great War (the First World War).

After the armistice of 1918 which ended the First World War, Europe was reshaped in the Paris peace conferences in a way reminiscent of Vienna in 1815. New countries were forged out of the German, Austrian, Turkish and Russian Empires, such as Czechoslovakia, Hungary and the Baltic states of Estonia, Latvia and Lithuania, while Poland reappeared for the first time since 1795. Once more, Europe was recast after an almighty war, which consigned the Vienna settlement to the annals of history just as it had done to the Treaty of Utrecht.

However, the century of peace that followed the Congress of Vienna was in marked contrast to the twenty-one-year truce that separated the end of the First World War from the start of the Second. Whatever the failings of the diplomats of 1815, their contribution to the peace that followed deserves some respect.

GLOSSARY

Absolute rule A system of government in a country in which the ruler has all the power.

Alliance Solidaire An idea put forward by Tsar Alexander I of Russia at the Congress of Aix-la-Chapelle in 1818 which was also known as the 'Universal Union'. It revived his earlier idea of the 1815 Holy Alliance but was not accepted.

Ancient frontiers/limits Normally this referred to France, and its frontiers of 1792, before it began its wars of conquest abroad under the Republic. (See also natural frontiers.)

Aristocracy The 200–300 most important decision-makers in a political system, which in the past mostly consisted of the nobility. (See also nobility.)

Autocracy A system of rule in a country that is led by an autocrat, someone who controls all power him or herself.

Balance of power The phrase used by the peacemakers at Vienna, in different ways, to describe what they saw as a fair redistribution of land primarily amongst themselves. It was intended that no one power would be able to dominate in future as France had. Priority was given to military and economic factors, but in no sense was it a precise formula.

Buffer state A small country lying next to a larger one, the role of which in wartime was to absorb the initial impact of an attack. Several of these linked together in 1815 to form the *cordon sanitaire*.

Carlsbad Decrees A series of measures put forward by Metternich and sanctioned by the Frankfurt Diet 1819–20 to prevent discussion of political ideas in Germany.

Concert of Europe The five great powers and their co-operation in the decades after 1815.

Constitution A set of rules for government, laying down the powers of each different part of it.

Continental System An economic blockade of Britain by Napoleon begun in 1806.

Cordon sanitaire A neutralised corridor along France's eastern frontier, composed of buffer states such as the Kingdom of the Netherlands and Piedmont.

Counter-factual history The analysis of history by deliberately omitting some evidence, to try to assess its impact. It is beloved by American historians who, for instance, asked if the cold war would have started if the USA had not dropped the atomic bomb.

Departement French administrative area, equivalent to an English county.

Eastern Question The problem of the future of the Turkish Empire, particularly in the nineteenth century.

Great power One of the five main states of Europe from 1815: Britain, Russia, Austria, Prussia and France.

Historiography The history of History and historians' views on the subject.

Holy Alliance A treaty put forward by Tsar Alexander I of Russia and signed in 1815 by almost all of the major European rulers in which they agreed to base their policies on Christian principles. It was not taken seriously until it was transformed into an instrument of repression by the Troppau Protocol, 1820.

Hundred Days The period of just over three months from 1 March 1815 to 18 June1815 when Napoleon returned to France from exile on Elba. He granted a liberal constitution but was beaten in the Battle of Waterloo.

Ideology A system of ideas, such as liberalism, nationalism, communism or fascism.

Legitimacy Restoration of royal and noble rulers to their pre-Napoleonic positions of power by strict hereditary right.

Liberalism The ideology of freedom. In nineteenth-century Europe, it was bound up with the rights and freedoms guaranteed in constitutions, or with economic freedom through *laissez-faire* or free trade.

Nationalism The ideology of a nation or a people having the right to rule itself. Defining the identity of a nation is extremely difficult, but is bound up with language and culture. Examples of nations that did not rule themselves in 1815 were Germans, Italians and Poles.

Napoleonic Wars   Wars fought by France under Napoleon from 1801. (See also revolutionary wars.)

Natural frontiers   A country's borders that are marked by geographical features, such as mountains or rivers. It has often been used in relation to France and the natural frontier it claimed for its own eastern border along the River Rhine which it wanted to reach.

Nobility   Peers. Those members of a society that hold a title such as Lord, Duke, Marquis or Earl.

Plenipotentiary   A diplomat who has the power to act independently on behalf of the government or ruling body.

Power vacuum   An area of land where government control is weak because it lacks the resources to make itself strong. The term was commonly applied to Germany in 1815 which was not at the time a country but a patchwork of small states.

Quadruple Alliance   A treaty signed by Britain, Russia, Prussia and Austria against France.

Revolutionary Wars   Wars fought by France after the Revolution of 1789 and before Napoleon came to power in 1800. (See also Napoleonic Wars.)

Romanticism   An early nineteenth-century cultural and political movement that was in part a reaction against the order and rationalism of the eighteenth century. It stressed the emotions and demanded a more impassioned approach to the arts and a deep commitment to a political cause (however futile it might be). At the Congress of Vienna, it was evident in the entertainment as a medieval joust, while in the years after 1815 it saw political expression amongst die-hard revolutionaries and in particular the band of volunteers who joined the Greek struggle for independence in the 1820s.

State Paper   Issued by Castlereagh 5 May 1820 to set out Britain's view on the balance of power and its own attitude towards rebellions in particular. Britain was content not to intervene so long as the overall balance was not upset; this was the 'fluid frontiers' approach to the balance of power.

Treaty of Kalisch   The most controversial area of debate between the great powers at the Congress of Vienna. It was signed by Russia and Prussia in 1813 and set out their aims for territorial gain in eastern Europe; Russia was to take Poland and Prussia was to take all of Saxony. In January 1815, they were both forced to settle for less, after the threat of war between the five great powers became a real danger.

Troppau Protocol Metternich's answer to the State Paper in which he set out the view adopted by Austria, Russia and Prussia – that they would intervene against rebellions to restore legitimate rulers; this was a 'fixed frontiers' approach to the balance of power.

Xenophobia Hatred of foreigners.

GLOSSARY OF PLACENAMES

This list is by no means comprehensive but aims to clarify some of the most common placenames, especially where the area is known by more than one name.

Austrian Netherlands   Eighteenth-century name for Belgium, when Austria ruled it.

Bessarabia   An area of land taken by Russia from Turkey in 1812 by the Treaty of Bucharest which lay on the eastern side of the River Danube's delta.

Congress Poland   Poland as constituted by the Congress of Vienna, in which Russia took all but Posen, Thorn and Galicia.

Grand Duchy of Warsaw   Napoleonic Poland.

Holy Roman Empire   The area that approximated to Germany from medieval times until its abolition by Napoleon in 1806.

Iberia   Spain and Portugal.

Kingdom of Naples   The southern half of the Italian peninsula and Sicily, also known as the Kingdom of the Two Sicilies.

Kingdom of Sardinia   The island of Sardinia and the mainland territory of Piedmont (with Genoa, Nice and Savoy from 1815).

Levant   Eastern end of the Mediterranean, both land and sea, from the French word *levant*, meaning to rise. It was from where the sun rose each day.

Piedmont   See Kingdom of Sardinia.

FURTHER READING

Most general textbooks on the nineteenth century have a chapter on the Congress of Vienna and sometimes one on the congress system as well. These provide an overview of the main events and some maps but lack the detail required for a full understanding of the subject. This pattern is usually repeated in the A-level topic books on the period.

By contrast, the books that specialise in the Congress of Vienna and its aftermath tend to be highly detailed studies of several hundred pages which most students of the period do not have time to read. Amongst these are C. Webster *The Congress of Vienna* (1919) and H. Nicholson *The Congress of Vienna* (1946). For the congress system, the most useful work is in H. Kissinger *A World Restored* (1973).

In addition, I have quoted from the following works (but would not necessarily recommend them to students, for the reasons given above: A.J.P. Taylor *The Course of German History* and *The Habsburg Monarchy*, and Wood *Europe 1815–1945*.

BIOGRAPHIES

This list of brief biographies is by no means comprehensive but gives a guide to leading figures in the creation and destruction of the Vienna settlement.

Alexander I As Tsar of Russia from 1801 to 1825, Alexander was responsible for the pursuit of war against Napoleon and, after allying with him from 1807–12, took a leading role in his defeat. It was the march to Russia in 1812 that caused Napoleon's downfall, as Alexander decided not only to retreat eastwards until Napoleon's army was exhausted but also to chase Napoleon back into western Europe beyond the frontiers of Russia, thus enabling Prussia and Austria to rejoin the fight.

At the Congress of Vienna, Alexander seemed to be going through a religious spell that led to him calling on fellow rulers to join together in a Christian fraternity for ruling Europe called the Holy Alliance. This impractical spiritual idea was widely endorsed by other monarchs before being conveniently ignored, because the Tsar's true aims seemed to be betrayed by a very traditional Russian desire to annex more land. He wanted to control all of Poland, which would allow a serious military threat to the central European powers; in the end he had to settle for 'Congress Poland' – most, but not all of Poland. In addition, Russia acquired Finland and Bessarabia.

Alexander himself did not forget the idea of Christian brotherhood so readily and revived it in 1818 at the Aix congress. By this time he termed it the *Alliance Solidaire*. It was shunned once more, but when it was converted to the Troppau Protocol by Metternich in 1820 the Holy Alliance became an effective instrument of repression along the lines of the Carlsbad Decrees in Germany. It promised to crush rebellions in minor states and the three eastern great powers were set to carry out the task.

While endorsing the policy in Italy, Alexander himself had difficulty with it in Greece where traditional Russian policies once more began to prevail as, although he disliked the uprising against Turkey, he hated the massacre of Christians, and yearned for a way to intervene. He was dissuaded by Metternich from doing so, but his death in December 1825 led to the appointment of Nicholas I and an immediate change of policy so as to help the Greeks. Inside Russia, Alexander took relatively little interest in reform, instead maintaining the autocracy during wartime and largely passing on the task of government after 1815 to Arakcheyev. This allowed him a much freer hand in foreign policy. What reforms there were tended to reinforce the power of the state, most notoriously the military colonies.

Bismarck, Count Otto von Bismarck was perhaps the main architect of the demise of the Vienna settlement as he set about expanding Prussian influence into north Germany and then into the whole of the 1815 German Confederation thereby creating the 'German Empire'. He came to power in Prussia as minister-president in 1862 having previously represented his country at the Frankfurt Diet and in the embassies of St Petersburg and Paris. He quickly established a reputation for himself as an ardent anti-liberal who stood outside of conventional political distinctions. However, he was committed to supporting his king, William I, and began as first minister when a crisis arose over the funding and modernisation of the Prussian army – a crisis that few others were prepared to take on.

His first moves in foreign policy were faltering as he was forced to distance himself from the Alvensleben Convention signed between Prussia and Russia in 1863 which would have helped in the brutal suppression of the Polish national uprising of the same year. He himself later claimed to have a 'master plan' for German unification, and in some respects this looks plausible. However, he used opportunities exceptionally well to out-manoeuvre his opponents.

This was shown by his exploitation of the Schleswig-Holstein crisis of 1864 which allowed him to annex Schleswig and then to engineer a war against Austria in 1866 which Prussia won. This enabled the annexation of several north German states and the creation of the North German Confederation which Prussia dominated. The war against France in 1870–1 provided sufficient nationalistic anti-French feeling to lift the south German states out of their regionalism and join the unified German state. His use of war owed much to the army reforms that he had first defended in order to come to power and, in conjunction with the Prussian industrial base, allowed him to enforce his policies through what came to be called *Realpolitik*. This was made possible too by the diplomatic realignment of the great powers after the Crimean War (1854–6) which had itself already ended the balance of power created at Vienna. However, Bismarck's policies confirmed the shift in power on the continent away from France to Germany.

Canning, George Canning took over the Foreign Office from Castlereagh in 1822 and instantly announced Britain's more isolationist policies. The difference in policy was more in tone than in substance, and Canning played upon his ability to woo public opinion, seeing foreign affairs as an issue behind which most voters (and the public at large) could unite. His speeches included memorable, if not altogether accurate, comments on British policies which stirred patriotic feelings.

In practice, he recognised the independence of the South American states, sent troops to Lisbon, Portugal, in 1826 to safeguard the constitution of the young queen and sent ships to Greece to support the Greek revolt against Turkey. His motives there were also to moderate Russian policies which under Tsar Nicholas I were bent on intervention. At the time of his death, all was well, but the sinking of the joint Turkish–Egyptian fleet by Codrington left the Turkish Empire unnervingly vulnerable to foreign aggressors in the eyes of the Foreign Office.

Castlereagh Viscount, second Marquess of Londonderry Castlereagh was one of the leading diplomats at the Congress of Vienna and the foremost advocate of a 'balance of power'. This was not so much an altruistic gesture for the peace and stability of the rest of Europe, as a means of ensuring Britain's own security for future years without committing Britain to open-ended involvement in European affairs. Britain looked for a fluid balance that allowed minor changes such as changes to rulers and frontiers in minor states, but was determined to resist any further French aggression. This was what lay behind his contribution to the Quadruple Alliance in which the great powers agreed to meet again at periodic intervals – the clearest reference to the congress system to emerge from the discussions of 1815. Thus, Castlereagh himself attended the first congress at Aix-la-Chapelle in 1818 as it dealt with France, but he soon distanced himself from the meetings as they merely became a forum for the repression of rebellions.

Castlereagh broke with his wartime allies in 1820 by issuing the famous State Paper which set out more than ever Britain's views. In it, he rejected the idea of actively maintaining a fixed balance of power. This view was answered by the Troppau Protocol which asserted the Holy Alliance powers' right to intervene in other countries' affairs, supposedly to uphold the balance of power but also to defend their own countries from possible unrest. Britain only sent an observer to the congresses after 1818 although Castlereagh had intended to go to the meeting at Verona since it dealt with the Eastern Question which he felt was a threat to the balance as a whole. His suicide in 1822 prevented this, and Canning gave new energy to Castlereagh's general policy of disengagement.

Cavour, Count Camillo di   Cavour was Prime Minister of the north Italian state of Piedmont (Sardinia) from 1851 to 1860 (with a brief six month respite during 1859). He was responsible for organising the war against Austria in 1859 that led to the annexation of Lombardy. In order to do this, he had to secure the support of Napoleon III, the leader of France, which he did in the secret negotiations held at Plombières in 1858. To make Piedmont a more attractive ally, he had spent the 1850s strengthening the economy by rebuilding the port of Genoa and starting the construction of the Mont Cenis tunnel through the Alps to France. The army was also built up and in 1859, it had 100,000 troops ready to fight. It was also Cavour's policy to invade the central Italian states of Parma, Modena, Tuscany and the Papal State of the Romagna while the war against Austria was under way. Thus, he hoped to create only a north Italian kingdom (an enlarged Piedmont) rather than a united Italy. He succeeded in his aim briefly in 1860, but was forced later in the year to accept the southern half of the peninsula from Garibaldi which effectively created a united Italy. This ended the Vienna settlement as Austrian influence was removed from all but the north east of the country and the petty rulers set up in 1815 fell.

Frederick William III   As King of Prussia 1777–1840, King Frederick William III guarded his small German state with considerable help from more able men than himself. In the late eighteenth century he took part in the Partition of Poland

and then joined in the wars against France during the 1790s. After the crushing defeat of Jena in 1806, he accepted that Prussia, an army with a state rather than a state with an army, was in need of modernisation. Stein ensured this happened and Prussian education, agriculture and military practices all improved; there was even a promise of a constitution, but this was not introduced. The effect was to make the administration more efficient and to make Prussia more defensible.

As part of the victorious Fourth Coalition against Napoleon, he attended the Congress of Vienna with his advisers chiefly with the aim of securing more land for Prussia so that its frontiers might become more easily defended. He allied with the Tsar of Russia in the Treaty of Kalisch so as to secure Saxony (in return for Russia taking all of Poland) but had to settle for less after war was threatened in 1815. Prussia was also saddled with the Rhineland, which at the time was a burden to bear as it was separated from the rest of Prussia's territory and put it in the front rank of states opposing any French attack. After 1815, he switched his allegiance to Austria so that, once again, Prussian security was assured. He followed Metternich's lead in Germany by endorsing the Carlsbad Decrees and fell into line with the Troppau Protocol of 1820. Under Frederick William III, Prussia did not use its troops, though, against any state after 1815.

Francis I   The Emperor of Austria from 1792–1835 largely gave up his role in foreign affairs to the much more able and talented Metternich. He accepted the policies of Metternich as they succeeded in keeping Austria amongst the great powers' inner circles and shored up the frontiers of an empire that he recognised was beginning to ail.

Garibaldi, Giuseppe   Garibaldi was an idealist who dreamed of a united Italy and who had the practical means to achieve it. As a Romantic, he never gave up his hope of seeing Italy unify but as a practical man he was ready to give up his republican ideas if the country stood a better chance of unifying under a monarch. This was what happened, as he gave up republicanism at some stage in the 1850s and fought a guerrilla war in 1860 against the King of Naples. With the help of 'The Thousand', his band of 'Red-shirts' he conquered first the island of Sicily and then the mainland territory of Naples. The 'Garibaldini' became the 'Army of the South' and was integrated into the Italian army after unification in 1860, just as his own conquests in the south were reluctantly accepted by Cavour in that year to join with the short-lived north Italian kingdom in the north. Thus, Garibaldi helped to end the 1815 settlement in Italy by bringing the southern half of the peninsula into the nascent state of Italy.

Louis XVIII   King of France, 1814–24. Louis was restored to the throne of France as a legitimate ruler not once but twice, the first time in 1814 and then again in 1815 after the Hundred Days. He ran away from Napoleon in March 1814 and had to be returned in the 'baggage train' of the allies. Consequently, his regime was associated with defeat and it lacked prestige. In the long run this contributed to the fall of the Bourbon dynasty in France in 1830 (under his brother, Charles X). However, Louis did what he could in difficult circumstances by ruling with moderation until 1820 and in particular he appointed the very talented Talleyrand to represent France at the Congress of Vienna where he succeeded in limiting the damage done to France. Unfortunately for France, the Hundred Days undid much of Talleyrand's work as it was punished in the Second Treaty of Paris.

Bourbon France recovered quite quickly after 1815 as the indemnity was paid off by 1818 and France was allowed to rejoin the concert of Europe in 1818 at Aix-la-Chapelle. Later, in 1823, French troops invaded Spain to restore the legitimate monarch, King Ferdinand, and this demonstrated that France was not only an independent great power but that it was anti-revolutionary. Within France, Louis' reign drifted towards more royalist policies after 1820 as he became increasingly frail and the right wing marshalled their forces following the assassination of the heir to the throne.

Metternich, Prince Clement   After a diplomatic career that took him to the eighteenth-century German courts as an ambassador, Metternich became minister of foreign affairs in 1809 and conducted foreign policy from then until he was dismissed in the revolutions of 1848. During this time, he ensured Austrian involvement in most of the diplomatic ventures of the period through his own dynamism and ingenuity. Joining the Fourth Coalition late so as not to desert Napoleon prematurely, he still managed to work with Castlereagh and the other allied leaders in defeating France and then arranging the peace negotiations for his own capital which gave him some advantages – in terms of administration and even to the point of emptying the foreign embassies' waste paper baskets so as to procure more information about their policy-making.

His aim of a 'just equilibrium' matched very closely Castlereagh's hopes of a 'balance of power' and the two men co-operated closely during the Congress of Vienna. This damaged Castlereagh's reputation in Britain where he was portrayed as being in league with continental reactionaries whose intention was to suppress all liberal movements. In fact, both men had their own state's security uppermost in their minds, especially with respect to Russia and France and it was this that guided their policies. Austria was vulnerable to attack from these two military heavyweights and it hoped to see them cancel each other out.

On a smaller scale, Metternich also wanted to stamp out threats to Austria that appeared as unrest in minor states. He therefore devised the Carlsbad Decrees and then the Troppau Protocol of 1820 so as to set out a framework for intervention against liberal revolts. His plans could not contain the basic drives behind other great powers, though, and this saw the end of co-operation with Castlereagh from circa 1820 and the independent action taken by Russia regarding the Eastern Question in the 1820s and 1830s. Throughout this period, though, he stifled political discussion in Germany and defended Austrian interests with great acumen.

Talleyrand, Charles Maurice de   It was Talleyrand who directed French foreign policy at the Congress of Vienna on behalf of Louis XVIII, having been instrumental in the restoration of the Bourbon monarchy. He was very successful in securing for France a full place in the negotiations at Vienna from January 1815 and thereby limiting the terms imposed on the country. He was fortunate in that the four allied great powers of Britain, Russia, Prussia and Austria fell out over the future of Poland and Saxony, but he exploited it to full effect and allied France to Britain and Austria in a temporary alliance. This brought the others to their senses, and a deal was quickly struck over Poland and Saxony, but it also meant that Talleyrand could defend French interests better and try to restrict Prussian gains on the River Rhine, for example. He tried to get support for a policy of legitimacy that would both remove all of the Napoleonic rulers, and defend French security by keeping the King of Saxony in power – which would once more limit Prussian gains.

After Napoleon's 'Hundred Days', much of Talleyrand's good work was undone as the French frontier was cut back and the nation was punished in the Second Treaty of Paris. However, he was to return in 1818 at the Congress of Aix-la-Chapelle and had the satisfaction of seeing the allied army of occupation leave French soil and the re-entry of France to the concert of Europe as a fully independent great power.

Wellington, Duke of This British military leader came to prominence during the Peninsular War in Spain and Portugal against Napoleon. By defeating the French army of occupation there, he was able to present Napoleon with war on two fronts by the time of his retreat from Moscow in 1813 and thus speed up the defeat of France. Most famously, he was the leader who ensured Napoleon's final defeat at Waterloo which ended the Hundred Days of rule that Napoleon had after his escape from Elba. In fact, he was helped considerably by the Prussian force under Blucher. In later years, he followed a political career with the British Tory Party and became, briefly, prime minister in 1828–30.

INDEX